Es

INDIA
and
AMERICA

Essays in Understanding

K.R. Narayanan

Published by

The Information Service of the
Embassy of India
Washington, D.C.

Copyright 1984: Embassy of India, Washington, D.C.

Contents

Foreword

One of the major goals of American foreign policy should be to bring about closer ties between the United States and other democracies, for whatever their differences such societies share the values of freedom of speech, of the press, and of governments which derive their legitimacy from the will of the people as expressed in free elections. One of the central aspects of United States policy must therefore be a sustained effort to develop better relations with India, the world's most populous democracy.

Ambassador K. R. Narayanan's diplomatic skills have made an important contribution to better Indo-American relations during the three years he has served as Indian ambassador to the United States. His obvious goodwill toward America, his intelligence, his ability to explain Indian policies in ways understandable to Americans, and his patience and determination in seeking areas of agreement and cooperation have played a major role in the steady progress our two countries have made in dealing with each other.

Ambassador Narayanan's activities in the United States have not, however, been confined to his official diplomatic duties. He has spoken publicly to a wide variety of audiences on Indian aspirations and problems, on the global issues confronting all nations in the late 20th century, and on the issues of education and human development as they affect all peoples. The speeches reprinted in this volume show him to be a man with an unusual breadth of view and a deep understanding of the human condition. They also convey his strong belief that there are universal human values and aspirations which are more important than historical and cultural differences, and that if the peoples of our two countries keep this perspective in mind we will find that we have only begun to realize the potential for closer and more fruitful Indo-American cooperation.

Stephen J. Solarz, Chairman
Subcommittee on Asian and Pacific
Affairs of the House Foreign
Affairs Committee

Preface

This volume is a selection from the many talks I have
had the opportunity to give at various institutions, associations and clubs in the United States during the last three
years. I was fortunate to get innumerable invitations to
speak. This enabled me, often together with my wife, to
travel extensively in this vast country, see something of its
infinite variety and experience the warm hospitality of its
people.

I am grateful to the World Affairs Councils, Foreign
Policy Associations, Universities, Women's organizations
and several clubs and groups in different parts of the
country for the facilities they afforded me to speak to their
members. The speeches were invariably followed by
question-and-answer sessions which were, actually, the more
exciting and profitable parts of my encounters with the
American public, but these could not be included in this
very restricted selection. In fact, only some of the speeches
were prepared and written out beforehand. More than half
of the speeches in this volume were given extempore, then
transcribed from tape recordings and edited for publication.

It was a pleasant surprise for me to find that despite the
common impression that for Americans India is a land of

'benevolent neglect', there was a great deal of interest in and goodwill for India though lying somewhat dormant in the minds and hearts of the people. I also found that one could talk frankly and argue openly with American audiences as long as one put across one's point of view in the spirit of friendship. At the same time I found that there exists something like a stock of misunderstandings and misconceptions, shared mutually by Americans as well as Indians, which has to be and can be overcome through patient and sustained contacts and exchanges between the people of the two countries.

I used to tell a story—a true story—to illustrate this peculiar mixture of goodwill and lack of understanding that characterises our relationship. A young American, who is now a distinguished professor in one of the universities in the U.S.A., spent some time in a village in Bihar in eastern India doing research on land reforms. When the time came for him to depart, the village panchayat, i.e. the village council, gave him a farewell reception. During the ceremonies and the speeches one of the members of the panchayat asked the village headman to find out from the chief guest whether there were water buffaloes in his country. When he answered "No" the member of the panchayat remarked that then it must be a poor country! Before the farewell function was over the puzzled young American was presented with two water buffaloes. The headman apologetically said that they could give only two buffaloes but they hoped that in course of time those would multiply and make America prosperous. This small incident illustrates two important points. One is the ignorance of the average Indian of America, an ignorance which, I think, is shared by the average American in regard to India. The second is the spontaneous goodwill that the ordinary Indian has for the American people. A buffalo for an Indian farmer is as or more precious than a tractor for an ordinary farmer in the United States and what the village panchayat in Bihar did was to give the young American the best that they had, a gift that posed for him a tricky practical problem. It would have been so if an American farmer had suddenly presented a small Indian peasant with a harvester-combine.

In the larger cultural, social and political fields there exist similar bottlenecks in understanding between our two countries. That is one of the reasons why I have called this collection "Essays in Understanding," essays not in the pedantic sense but in the sense of "efforts" or "attempts." As Congressman Stephen Solarz has pointed out in the "Foreword," India and America have "only begun to realize the potential" for a deeper understanding and fruitful cooperation. The development of this potential is a noble goal. I am fortunate to have got an opportunity to play a small and transient role in this process.

K. R. Narayanan
December 1983
Washington, D.C.

I
Indo-U.S. Ties:
An Adventure in Understanding

It has become a truism to say that Indo-U.S. relations have been marked by ups and downs or by alternating periods of warmth and coolness. Perhaps it is more correct to say that some sort of duality has existed at the core of this relationship. I am tempted to describe Indo-U.S. relationship as "half full of cold, half full of fire" in the words that the Spanish poet Lorca applied to a woman in one of his lyrics. The task of diplomacy, or rather statesmanship, is to mix the hot and cold and to generate a health-giving even temperature in our relationship that is neither frigid nor feverish.

Whatever be the ups and downs, and zigs and zags in Indo-U.S. relations, certain common things stand like stone—durable and fundamental. Individualism with the attendant urge for freedom and liberty is one of the inherent characteristics of both Americans and Indians, even though the expression of individualism is different in one society that is new and bursting with energy, and in the other that is ancient, complex and variegated. The intellectual and

Address on Indo-U.S. Relations at The Foreign Policy Association, New York, on May 3, 1982.

1

philosophical links between India and the United States have never been sufficiently examined or understood in the superficial passion for political interpretation and mis-interpretation. Ideas have travelled from India to America and from America to India influencing thought and action in both our countries. Great American thinkers and writers like Emerson, Thoreau and Walt Whitman were influenced by Indian philosophy, and they in turn profoundly in-fluenced both thinking and action in India through their writings and through great Indians like Swami Viveka-nanda, Tagore, Gandhi and Nehru. Besides, as Jawaharlal Nehru acknowledged during his first visit to the United States "an echo of the great voices of the founders of the American Republic" can be recognized in the Constitution and the political system of India.

This intellectual relationship has been facilitated by the English language and educational systems that are akin to each other. Students, scholars and professionals from India come to the United States in greater number than to any other foreign country weaving a network of personal relations between the U.S. and almost every part of India. The Indian community in this country, which is over 360,000 strong, comes from the educated cream of Indian society which is able not only to adapt to conditions in this far-away land of opportunity, but to contribute signifi-cantly to the professional, scientific and technological fields of development in this country. Though it constitutes a brain-drain from India, it can also be looked upon as a brain-bank abroad in which India is investing for the future. While these intellectual and cultural ties are facts, it must also be pointed out that there is a cultural gap separating the new society of the United States and the old civilization of India. For most Americans, India is still an exotic and sordid land of poverty, disease and squalor inundated by a ceaseless torrent of babies, while for most Indians, imbibing images from Hollywood and the media, America is an admirable and amazingly rich land, almost indecently affluent and materialistic, afflicted by crime, violence and sex. Here is a major cultural bottleneck in understanding, a bottleneck that exists in respect of life, society and politics.

The economic and commercial ties that bind our two countries are strong and growing. India's agricultural and industrial development has reached a stage today when it is possible for us to attract and absorb increasing investments from the U.S.A., particularly with the current liberalization of investment and trade policies by the Government of India. Our reservoir of scientific and technological personnel which is the third largest in the world, together with the sophisticated and diversified industrial infrastructure that has been built up offers opportunities for economic collaboration in India as well as in third countries between Indian and American enterprises. The Indian market is a steadily expanding market which can offer outlets to American capital, equipment and consumption goods even when some of the other lucrative markets of today might dry up or be closed. For India, the United States is a source of high technology and capital, and a market for its traditional as well as new industrial and engineering products. In the relationship between the United States, which represents the peak of economic and technological advance, and India, which is the paragon of a developing country, is telescoped not only a bilateral equation of major proportions, but the crucial economic relationship of our time viz. the North-South relationship. How we adjust our relations in the bilateral field to our mutual benefit might well point the way to the larger structural adjustment between the developed and the developing worlds.

It would be less than graceful on my part if I do not acknowledge here the great contribution that the United States has made to Indian economic development. From 1951 to 1971 it has been estimated that the U.S.A. gave India loans and grants to the tune of over $9 billion including 40 million tons of foodgrains. Today the level of assistance is infinitely smaller, contributing four to five percent of the total external assistance that India receives. The most glorious chapter in Indo-American economic-cum-technological cooperation has been written in the field of agriculture. India's Green Revolution and the basic self-sufficiency in foodgrains that we have achieved today owes a great deal to this cooperation.

In the field of international relations, notwithstanding our over-publicised differences, no two countries have a greater stake in the maintenance of world peace and the world balance and in the preservation of peace and stability in the vast Asian region. Our perceptions of the world may differ, and there are differences in our methods and approaches to international problems, but there is a basic thrust of commonality in our objectives, be it in the field of economics, politics, or international relations.

I have referred earlier to the intellectual and philosophical affinity between our two countries and peoples. This is symbolised by the one word 'democracy.' The significance of this democratic affinity has not been fully appreciated, and certainly not been integrated into practical policy-making. For India the fact that the United States is the greatest democracy and the most powerful nation in the world is of fundamental significance. The United States is a major factor in the world environment in which Indian democracy could develop and flourish. But I should submit that Indian democracy also holds significance for the U.S.A. and the world. To appreciate this it is necessary to ask the question why and how this system, which was handed over by the British in a rudimentary form to countries over which they held sway, survived and advanced in India, while it went down in many other countries before military coups and dictatorships. It has also to be understood that what has happened in India was not a mere imitation of a Western system, but the adaption of it to our conditions and needs, and the application of it to a massive process of socio-economic development and transformation. We are conscious of the difficulties and perils that face our democratic system, but the fact of six general elections involving a colossal electorate, the fact of changes of government, parties and leaders through the process of free elections, and the audacious application of the democratic method to basic social and economic development, are noteworthy in spite of all the deficiencies and shortcomings involved in the working of the system.

The British, though they introduced elements of the parliamentary system into India, were highly sceptical of the applicability of democracy in Indian conditions. Even today there are many in the West who look upon Indian democracy as some sort of transient illusion like the Indian rope trick, while the ideological East perhaps misconceives it as just a stage in what they consider to be the inexorable march towards Communism. But the fact is that in grappling with the great issues of Indian life, society, economy and politics, democracy has already moved from an experiment to an established system in India. To put a question mark against it, and to believe that only the elite of Western Europe and America are able to operate a democratic system, is to introduce a basic uncertainty into our relationship. I should like to make here a related point. If the Western connection has facilitated India to emerge as a democratic nation, would it be possible, in a world of intense ideological and power contest, and in a world where the majority of mankind lives and struggles in the vast region of the developing countries, for the Western countries to flourish in the long-run as islands of democracy and affluence, without at least some countries, certainly a populous and strategic landmass like India, remaining a political democracy and an example of social and economic development through democratic means? I feel that in this particular field it is possible for populous and developing India, and rich and powerful America to help and reinforce each other. This does not mean that we should get together in some sort of crusade for democracy through a global ganging-up. We believe that our political and our value-systems can be protected without such lining-up; indeed, to do so would be, in our judgement, more destructive than supportive of our democracy, as the real threats to it are internal rather than external, and have to be dealt with by political, social and economic methods rather than by weapons and military methods.

It is necessary to understand this democratic, peaceful strategy of development adopted by India if one is to appreciate the policy of nonalignment which is integrally related to it. Nonalignment has been the single issue over which Indo-U.S. understanding got confounded, and most of our differences in international relations can be traced to the confusion over this basic issue. Now, nonalignment is a relatively new concept and approach in international politics. It is not neutrality, which is essentially a war-time concept, but a strategy for peace, and its principal objective is not so much to enable neutrality in the event of war as to lessen tensions and to avert war itself.

John Foster Dulles had mistaken nonalignment for neutrality and condemned it as " immoral." Dante had written in his classical work that a special part of hell was set apart for those who remain neutral on the great issues of life. Jawaharlal Nehru had echoed the same sentiment when he told the U.S. Congress in 1949 that when freedom is threatened and justice menaced, India cannot and shall not be neutral. That approach, however, did not imply that we would line up with others and plunge into cold war. In modern politics, the dividing line between heavenly hosts and Satanic forces has become somewhat thin, and the black and white view of the world is no longer valid. Today the predicament of humanity is such that if there is a world war, be it for the noblest of causes, both the righteous and the wicked would find themselves in the hell of fire and brimstone and atomic radiation. It was in this context that Jawaharlal Nehru put forward his policy of nonalignment and peaceful co-existence warning that the alternative to co-existence was only "co-destruction."

If Dulles could not appreciate nonalignment, so could not others in more recent times, which perhaps, is not an isolated individual difficulty but a reflection of the general attitude towards this rather new-fangled policy. In his 'White House Years' Dr. Henry Kissinger refers to India "as a country which had distanced itself from most of our foreign policy objectives in the name of nonalignment." At another place in the same book he showed a better understanding of the policy, but in a manner that ignored Indian interests and sensitivities. "Just as our wooing for two decades," Dr. Kissinger writes, "had not managed to tempt India out of its nonalignment, so India was unlikely to move irrevocably to one side as a result of our defending our own interests (the reference here is to U.S. "tilt" towards Pakistan during the Bangladesh crisis). Nonalignment enables India to navigate the international passage with a maximum number of options. For that reason we were convinced that India would sooner or later seek a rapproachment with us again if only to keep Moscow from taking it for granted."

The implication of all this is that India, in order to maintain its nonaligned foreign policy, would get along with the United States, even if the United States hurt India. Strangely, we have heard the same line of argument during the recent discussion on the supply of arms to Pakistan, viz. that India might fret and fume for some time, but would desist from doing anything that would jeopardise Indo-American relations. Perhaps, there are some in India also who think along the same lines in regard to the U.S.A.'s relations with India (but not at the official level and certainly not in the recent past) and believe that one can criticize the United States without damaging our basic relations with it. But arms, F-16s and nuclear ships are more concrete and dangerous things than words and criticisms. I think the worst thing in Indo-American relations is to take each other for granted. Even when there are no immediate and vehement reactions, one must take into account the slow, incremental re-adjustments in foreign policy generated by such policies and actions.

The most conspicuous as well as pervasive misunderstanding between India and America centre around the Soviet Union, and hence it is important to examine this closely and realistically. Prime Minister Mrs. Gandhi has often stated that she is neither pro-Soviet nor pro-America, but simply pro-Indian. We are certainly friendly to the Soviet Union. It is commonsense to seek friendship with a neighbour, especially with a neighbour that is a super power, that has not hurt the interests of India, but on the other hand has extended support to us in some very critical situations. It would be foolish if we adopted an unfriendly attitude towards such a neighbour on ideological or cold-war considerations. Our friendship with the Soviet Union has not affected our internal political and social system, nor has it constricted the pursuit of friendly relations with any other country including the United States, Western Europe, Pakistan, and China, and the nonaligned countries. It was one of the nonaligned maxims of Jawaharlal Nehru that India's friendly relations with one country should not come in the way of friendly relations with any other country. Mrs. Indira Gandhi has often stated that India's policy is to try to lessen hostility where there is hostility, to increase friendship where there is friendship. In this context I should like you to consider what the situation in our region would have been if India had joined a strategic combination or consensus against the Soviet Union. It would have resulted in India and the region being drawn into great-power rivalries and conflicts, turning it into an area of contention and in-security. In that event would it have been possible for the United States to continue its stance of benevolent neglect of India giving it a low priority in its strategic pre-occupations?

The charge that India is pro-Soviet needs further probing in view of its pervasive influence on American thinking. There seems to be a psychological penumbra surrounding this thinking. As early as January 1947, ten months before India became independent, John Foster Dulles made a statement that "in India Soviet Communism exercises a strong influence through the Interim Govern-ment." This statement was made when Lord Mountbatten was the Governor of India and Nehru the Vice-President of the Interim Government. It is a little surprising that in a booklet entitled "Soviet Military Power" published in May 1981, India has been shown along with Cuba, Ethiopia, Yemen, etc. as a country where exist "major concentrations of Soviet and East European Military Advisers." Such perceptions do violence to facts. From the Indian side it would be equally erroneous if we thought that behind these perceptions there does not exist understanding and friendship for India in America, and if we believed that the United States is unmindful of the need for coexistence and has embarked upon a collision course with the Soviet Union. We do appreciate the fears, suspicions and the sense of insecurity of the United States, and we also know that there are such fears in Moscow as well. One of the objectives of non-alignment is to contribute, to whatever small degree possible, to the overcoming of this wall of fear and suspicion that divide the super powers.

The international outlook of our two countries has heavily influenced our bilateral relations. As a matter of fact there are no clashes of interests between us in the bilateral field in an intrinsic sense. It is the focusing of the global approach on bilateral issues that has magnified into major differences some of the bilateral issues. That is so with regard to differences over the supply of nuclear fuel for the Tarapur plant and arms supplies to Pakistan. With regard to Tarapur, a valid international agreement, every clause of which India has strictly observed, has been rendered unworkable owing to developments in American policy on nuclear nonproliferation and American domestic legislation well after the agreement was signed. Both sides have expressed willingness to have the problem settled in an amicable manner avoiding negative fall-out on our general, friendly relations.

On Pakistan it is not often understood that, notwith-standing our differences and conflicts with that country, we have great stake in Pakistan's integrity and stability than any other nation and that ever since partition it has been our endeavor to heal the wounds and evolve a relationship of friendship and co-operation with this neighbour. For various reasons we have not achieved success in this so far. The drawing of Pakistan into a military alliance system and the consequent militarization of Pakistani politics are not irrelevant to the failure of the two countries to come closer together. As in the past the present supply of arms to Pakistan is in the cold war context and linked to a global strategic consensus. Whether the United States wanted it or not, this would not only raise tensions in the region, but also pose a threat to India's security and national interest. In addition it is likely to interfere with the improvement of relations between India and Pakistan, and its repercussions in Pakistan itself can well be negative. To my mind what is involved in this Pakistan policy is not only unawareness or under-estimation of the consequences, but a mistaken strategic doctrine that Pakistan is the defensive bastion in the region. While we in India appreciate U.S. concerns over developments in the region, and we stand for the with-drawal of Soviet troops from Afghanistan, we believe that the objectives that all of us have in view cannot be achieved without talks and negotiations leading to a political settle-ment. The stand that India has taken in regard to the Afghanistan situation is calculated to help such a process sooner or later. I should like to add here that notwith-standing our differences with the United States in the approach to the Afghan question and on arms to Pakistan, I have no doubt that we can together overcome these hindrances and improve our relations; and as regards Pakistan, we are determined to go ahead with our efforts for improvement of relations.

From Korea to Afghanistan American dissatisfaction with Indian foreign policy has been that we have not sided with it or used sufficiently strong condemnatory language against the Soviet Union. In regard to some of these crises India had actually played a role that was helpful to the U.S.A. and to world peace, and though misunderstood at the time, it was recognized later as events unfolded themselves. For a global power, a different approach by another country on global issues might be somewhat irritating. But that ought not to be interpreted as being contrary to the vital interest of the United States, unless it is believed that if a country does not line up with you it is against you. There is room for honest differences as to how to approach critical international questions, and such differences in approach need not necessarily be blown up into major bilateral rifts. At any rate, it ought to be appreciated that some of the issues on which India has differences with the U.S.A. like the policy towards Pakistan, supply of technologically advanced arms and equipment to Pakistan, are such that they adversely and seriously affect India's vital national and security interest. The basic affinities and the common interests that link our two great nations are so fundamental and over-riding that it has been possible for us to overcome even these and maintain our friendship and co-operation. But if we could understand each other's mental processes, politcal and economic compulsions, and geostrategic situations a little more intensely and in greater depth, it would be possible for us to avoid most of the misunderstandings and zigs and zags in our relationship. To my mind, Indo-U.S. relations are less an exercise in the resolution of problems and disputes, even though there are problems that must be resolved, than an adventure in mutual understanding.

II
Democracy and Economic Development

George Bernard Shaw once said that England and America were two countries separated by the same language. In a similar lighthearted vein one might say that India and the United States are two countries separated by the same political system.

We are both democracies, the two largest in the world, sharing common human values, political principles and free electoral processes. But, we are also two democracies that function in geographical, historical, cultural and developmental contexts that are vastly different. Jawaharlal Nehru, the first Prime Minister of India, used to say that the world would look different depending on from where you looked at it, from New Delhi, Washington, Moscow or London. It is, therefore, natural that our perceptions of the world and our approaches to problems may differ, though in the realm of fundamental objectives and larger interests, we are linked by over-informing affinities. This, to my mind, is precisely the type of relationship that calls for efforts at understanding, as the differences do not arise from conflicts of

Speech to the Commonwealth Club of California, 23rd March 1983.

13

interests and objectives, but from bottle-necks in understanding. That is probably why Prime Minister Mrs. Indira Gandhi, during her visit to the United States last year, emphasized the theme of understanding and described her own visit as "an adventure in friendship and understanding."

It is particularly difficult for an advanced, affluent, and powerful nation to understand fully the hopes, the fears, and the sensitivities of a developing nation, struggling to uplift from poverty millions of its people, and seeking to promote around it, and in the wider world, an atmosphere of peace and tranquility, by following a policy of nonalignment and peaceful co-existence. Besides, there are the established images of India to be overcome, images disseminated during the colonial period, of an India hopelessly divided into jarring regional, religious and linguistic groups, and an India that is irredeemably poverty-stricken, static, stagnant and backward. These images are too deeply imbedded in the minds of people to be erased easily, especially when much of the reporting in the media is often sensationally negative.

In a supplement on India two years ago, the London "Economist" wrote as follows:

"India has always been a fashionable object of gloom. Since Independence each decade has thrown up a new threat to the country's foundations. In the 1940s it was communal violence. In the 1950s secession was supposedly in the air. . . . under the strain of regional and linguistic rivalries. In the 1960s the life-boat theory of a planet doomed by Malthusian shortages, cast India as the natural candidate for being chucked over-board, the better to save others. In the 1970s, the Emergency seemed to confirm long-standing doubts that India could be governed democratically. On all counts, the pessimists have been wrong."

But pessimism about India continues to persist. Some of the problems are still with us, but in minor and manageable forms. What is remarkable is that India, with all its differences, has consolidated itself as a stable and united political entity, and is today a rapidly changing, developing economy. It has weathered successfully many a fissiparous threat to its unity, and demonstrated its age-old genius of accommodating and reconciling differences, and living together in peace and co-existence, notwithstanding occasional eruptions of social, economic or political trouble in one part or another of this vast country. The major fact is that seven massive general elections have been held since Independence, involving the largest free electorate in the world, and state, district, municipal and village elections are held from time to time, as part of the normal political life of the people. India has managed some very critical transitions in political power, through peaceful democratic means making democracy in India no longer an experiment, but an established fact. Impressed with this phenomenon some perceptive observers have remarked that, for India, diversities are a source of strength rather than of weakness. But the old habit of scepticism and pessimism about India still persists, as if our demonstrable stability and democracy are not actual realities, but some kind of an illusory Indian rope-trick.

One may ask what India has really achieved in the economic and social field? We are no doubt still bedevilled by social and economic ills and deprivations, and our progress may not look very impressive in comparison with the high levels of affluence attained by developed countries like the United States. The appropriate comparison is, however, with our own past. During the glorious days of the British Empire, India was the victim of periodic famines every twenty-five or thirty years, sometimes even more frequently, the last of which in the Province of Bengal took a toll of three million lives in 1942. It is this India that is today self-sufficient in foodgrains, and is estimated by foreign experts to be capable of becoming even a food-exporting nation in the future. This green revolution, as we call it, has been achieved, not by collectivising farms and dislocating vast numbers of rural people, but peacefully, and by giving greater freedom and initiative to the farmer, and through a scientific-technological breakthrough in agriculture, in which agricultural specialists from the U.S.A. played a crucial and beneficial role. We have yet to provide adequate nutritional standards in the diet of our people, but to have attained basic self-sufficiency in food-grains production, when population almost doubled since Independence is an achievement that has not made any image-making impact in the United States, probably because it was silent and peaceful progress and not a dramatic, and violent revolution.

The industrial development of India has been equally remarkable. From the position of almost an industrial zero at the time of Independence, India has now emerged as the 10th largest industrial nation in the world with the third largest pool of scientific-technical-managerial skills in the world, coming only after the USA and the USSR. India now produces almost all the consumption goods basically needed by our people, and also manufactures tractors, motor cars, railway locomotives and wagons, electric power stations and transmission lines, fertilizer and steel factories, ships including passenger liners and bulk carriers, aircraft, satellites etc. The industrial infrastructure that has been built up is sophisticated and variegated. The country nevertheless remains predominantly rural and agricultural. But already the change brought about through industrialisation is striking, with appropriate technology spreading to rural areas, with agro-industries, small scale and middle scale enterprises coming up rapidly, giving rise to a new middle class of entrepreneurs and businessmen full of initiative and dynamism. Twenty-five percent of our domestic product is accounted for by industrial production, and 60% of our exports, previously dominated by traditional agricultural commodities and raw materials, is now composed of manufactured goods. There has also emerged a modern sector of the economy 100 million strong with capacity to expand further. There is thus in India an advanced economic base and an expanding sophisticated market of considerable size that provides promising prospects for trade, commerce and investment for American businessmen and industrialists.

I should like to draw your attention to two or three general indicators of India's social and economic progress. During the last 50 years of British rule the rate of growth of India's GNP was hardly one percent, revealing the stagnation in economic development. Since Independence we have managed an average annual rate of growth of 3.5 to 4 percent, touching sometimes to 8 percent and maintaining during the last three years an average of five percent. The other indicator is the significant increase in the average expectation of life of an Indian from 33 years in 1951 to 53 years in 1981. Robert McNamara described this rate of increase in life expectancy as unprecedented in history. In this piece of statistics is telescoped the very substantial and comprehensive social and economic development of India during the first thirty years—in agriculture, in industry, in science and technology, in education, health, medical and social services. I should like to add two more indicators. Population growth, which has been staggering especially in absolute terms, has been stabilised and stands at 1.9 to 2.0 percent at present with prospects of further lowering of the rate, and that when the death rate has gone down rather significantly. The other point to be noted is the bringing down of inflation from 20 percent to 4.7 percent within a period of three years.

The message of this economic development of India has begun to get across to people in the United States. But the image of India as a centrally-controlled socialist economy, where private enterprise is handcuffed and stifled, and where foreign investment is restricted, persists. The fact is that India has throughout followed not doctrinaire but pragmatic policies, while paying heed to the demands of social justice and equity, and the need for the state to manage some of the commanding heights of the economy, like heavy industries and public utilities.

Early in the 1960s Professors Millikan and Rostow from Harvard wrote as follows in regard to India: "There are situations in which development must already be firmly established, before it is reasonable to expect private investment to take primary initiative, for pushing it forward. In such situations insisting that investments must be wholly or largely privately administered from the start, may prevent preconditions for private investment being established." In fact, the Marxist critique of India's developmental strategy has been that it has enabled the public sector to facilitate the growth of the private sector. Today only 20 percent of India's domestic product is contributed by the public sector, 80 percent is in private hands including the entire field of agriculture, and small scale and medium scale industries, and some big industries as well. Private enterprise in India is today experiencing new opportunities for expansion, but within the larger framework of public policy, and in accordance with the basic priorities, combining development with social justice.

The new economic liberalisation policy of the Government of India has emerged as an evolution from the totality of India's agricultural and industrial advance, quickened by new needs and circumstances, and responding to the requirements and challenges of the new stage of the development of the economy. It is not a retreat from the country's basic economic philosophy and strategy, but rather a charging forward from an economic base already established and secured. For that reason the new liberalisation will be an enduring and expanding phenomenon.

In the field of trade the United States is, for India, already the largest partner with 10 percent of its exports going to the USA and 12 percent of its imports coming from it. Since 1977 our two-way trade has doubled and now stands at three billion dollars. It is rather small, considering the potentialities, but I believe that it would be eminently practicable to double the volume of trade in the next three to five years taking advantage of the new liberalization of imports and the vigorously pursued new programme of exports.*

Equally important is the liberalisation of the investment climate in India today. Mr. Craig A. Nalen, President of OPIC who led a delegation to India recently—the largest

---

*Latest figures show that the volume of trade between India and the United States during the first six months of 1983 has reached the three billion dollar mark, indicating the possibility of a doubling of trade during 1983.

private enterprise delegation that has ever gone to any country from here—described the investment climate in India as "highly favourable" and the country as "a promising area for U.S. private investment." During the last two to three years, investment rules, regulations and procedures have been streamlined and simplified in India. Further, in addition to the 40% equity participation allowed for foreign investment, there could now be 50 to 75% equity participation in high technology areas, and even up to 100% equity shares in export oriented industries. As a matter of fact between 1980 and 1982 U.S. investments in India grew from $396 million to $500 million. The size of this investment is not large enough, but the recent rates of growth point to the potentialities in the future.

Indo-American joint ventures in India tell a remarkable success story not very well known. A study of 34 Indo-U.S. joint ventures has shown that they have increased their turnover steadily and significantly, earning 20.3% net profits after tax, and dividends of 14.8% for the repatriation of which there are absolutely no hindrances. Out of 6500 foreign collaboration agreements in existence, 1200 are with the U.S.A. During the last two years, the U.S.A. has obtained the largest number of industrial collaboration licenses overtaking Britain in this respect. A new feature is joint ventures in third countries. Referring to India's new liberalisation policy, Mr. Orville Freeman, Chairman of Business International, said: "The implications of the new strategy are staggering. If pursued steadily and vigorously, it could propel India's take-off into the ranks of the major economic powers, not in some distant vision, but in the foreseeable future."

The continuance and the success of the new Indian liberalisation strategy would depend, however, on two major external factors. One is that the current trend in developed countries, including the United States, towards protectionism should be arrested so that Indian exports could enter the U.S. and the developed markets of the world. The second is that the concessional financial flows from international multi-lateral banking institutions, of which india has been a major beneficiary, should continue uninterrupted. Any sizeable reduction of this flow will adversely affect India's balance of payments and economic developments and, inevitably, the new liberalisation policies as well. It is a question impinging not only upon India but the entire developing world. The great developed countries will have to think in the long term, and in a big way, on the problems of the South where the majority of mankind lives, where much of the discontents and the restlessness of the world are generated, and where the huge markets of the future are.

In the beginning of this address I referred to the need for understanding. Democracy is the basis as well as the framework of Indo-U.S. understanding and cooperation. Between us a mere cash nexus, however significant, is not sufficient to sustain our relationship. Even our trade and economic relations are founded on the commonality of values and ideas, and on philosophical and intellectual links connecting us. The educational systems in our two countries are very much akin to one another which is one of the reasons why so many Indians have come to this country as students, teachers, professionals, scientists, technologists and businessmen, improving their fortunes and making some contributions to development here. There have been in the past active exchanges of scholars and students between the two countries in a variety of fields. The American Institute of Indian Studies, for example, has created and fostered a network of relationships between India and the United States in the areas of business, the humanities, social sciences and the performing arts. These days industry, commerce and business encompass a wide spectrum of human relations. It is important, therefore, that for the promotion of economic relations, the work of institutions like the American Institute of Indian Studies as well as University studies on India are encouraged. That would provide an intellectual-cultural content to economic cooperation, and a deeper and a subtler basis for understanding between our two great democracies.

III

Nonalignment Today: The New Delhi Summit

Nonalignment is a somewhat difficult and elusive subject to talk about. I am gladdened by the good turnout at this meeting. It has been my experience during my travels in this country that whatever the media might say, there is considerable interest among people in this idea of nonalignment. That is especially so after the New Delhi Summit Conference. It may be because this policy reflects the aspirations of people all over the world for peace and for living together on this planet of ours.

The Prime Minister of India, Mrs. Gandhi, described nonalignment as the "biggest peace movement in the world." I think this is a very appropriate description. When we say peace movement we do not mean any kind of sectarian type of movement, but the desire and the struggle of people everywhere in the world, including in the aligned countries, for a more peaceful world.

I should like to make a few observations regarding the origins and the background of nonalignment. First and foremost one could say that anti-colonialism or anti-imperialism is the birthmark of nonalignment. Mrs. Gandhi

Address to the India Council of Washington, D.C. on March 29, 1983.

23

pointed out in her inaugural address at the Delhi summit
that almost all the nonaligned countries of today came to
this policy out of the colonial experience they had gone
through, either directly or indirectly. Therefore when one
analyses and judges the resolutions and statements coming
out of nonaligned conferences it would be good to remem-
ber this, because no nonaligned gathering will be able to
discard this basic birthmark. It will always be there in their
rhetoric, in their policies and struggles. Unless this is
appreciated I think there could be no real understanding of
nonalignment. Even though the United States of America
has been one of the first anti-colonialist countries in the
world, today having become a major power, a super power,
it tends to forget its past. It is possible that when we have
realized in practice for all countries a world that is more
equal, more just and more affluent, the nonaligned countries of today will not think so much about their anti-
colonial origins. But until then this must be accepted as a
basic characteristic of the movement.

The second point—and this was also emphasized by
Prime Minister Indira Gandhi in her inaugural address—is
that the movement is based on the desire to keep away from
the conflicts of the aligned nations which, as Nehru put it,
produced many wars in the past and which might lead to
wars on an even larger scale in the future. That is the
rationale of not being aligned to any bloc—military or
ideological. This aspect of nonalignment represented a
search by the new emerging nations for a different world
order. They were not moved by big ambitions to turn the
world upside down. What they tried to formulate was a new
system or alternative system of relations among nations that
would not be based, as it was in the past, on power politics
or the balance of power which have their reincarnations

today in concepts like "mutually assured destruction," "massive retaliation," "nuclear deterrence," etc.

The nonaligned nations have tried to emphasize not so much the play of power in the international field—though naturally they recognized the existence of power and its importance in the world—but to search for new avenues of settling disputes peacefully. They put enormous emphasis on the process of negotiations and on the inevitability of co-existence in this world among different ideological, military, political and social systems.

Even before the Belgrade Conference of 1961, non-alignment had become a well-known policy. It had already become an international grouping of a very loose kind, though confined to Asia at that time. The earliest foreign policy moves of India, which produced some results, whether it was in Korea or Indochina, or later in the Congo, or in the Lebanon, were based on the approach and policy of nonalignment. In Asia there came together a group of nations, a very small group consisting of India, Burma, Indonesia and Sri Lanka, and also Pakistan (until it joined western military pacts) which more or less formed what was known at that time as the Southeast Asia pattern. India, Burma and Indonesia formed the nucleus of this inter-national expression of nonalignment in Asia. I think the Colombo Conference of 1954 was the peak point of this informal grouping. Later it blossomed in a different way at Bandung in 1955 as the Afro-Asian Conference though strictly it was not a gathering of the nonaligned. What took place in Belgrade in 1961 was a formalization and a broadening of a movement which already existed in Asia. The emergence of Yugoslavia as a leading nonaligned nation was a major point of departure that projected the movement onto Europe and through Europe onto the international field as a whole. The importance of Belgrade was that it was there that nonalignment was projected on the world state as an international force.

There occurred a rapid growth of the movement since 1961—as you know there were 25 nations in Belgrade and there were 101 nations in New Delhi. Almost every country that attained its freedom after the Second World War moved into the nonaligned fold. The exceptions have been very few. Thus almost literally nonalignment was an emergence from colonialism.

When the nonaligned nations meet they are of course aware of the great powers and their power, and of the struggle between different ideologies and military systems; it is, however, not with the struggle of these powers that they are obsessed but with the search for peace, co-existence, disarmament and development. Therefore, when people sitting in newspaper offices or government offices in aligned countries try to count the number of times the United States or the Soviet Union or any other country was mentioned in the final documents of the nonaligned, they are adopting a wrong approach. If any country is mentioned, it is because such mention arises logically and circumstantially from the problems that the movement and the world face, not because the movement wishes to keep some sort of strict balance between East and West or tilt to one side or the other. Nonalignment is not neutrality; its main preoccupation is with the basic common problems of the countries comprising the movement, their hopes, aspirations and fears, making their own analysis of the world situation and judging for themselves what could promote world peace generally and bring about peaceful solutions to problems in different parts of the world.

Therefore, at these nonaligned conferences people are

not fixing their eyes on Washington or Moscow, trying now to keep an even balance between the two. Though they take into account the power factors in the world and pay due regard to the great powers, they look at every issue, first of all, on its merits, secondly, in the general circumstances of the problem, its origins and its present manifestation, thirdly, as it affects the common interests of the countries of the movement as a whole, and fourthly, but not least importantly, on the basis of the requirements of world peace as seen by them. This is really the rationale behind the formulations and declarations of the movement.

There is a convention that bilateral differences among nonaligned countries are not discussed at nonaligned conferences. They may be mentioned by one country or another, but they are not discussed for the simple reason that we want to focus attention on major issues affecting the nonaligned and the larger issues which encompass the fate of mankind as a whole.

Jawaharlal Nehru said as early as 1961 in Belgrade, and there were furious attacks on him when he said it, that the era of classical colonialism was dead, and that the nonaligned had to give greater attention to vital issues of war and peace. Nehru did not actually mean that colonialism was no longer a problem, but that it was on the retreat—though there were various new manifestations of it. After all, the essence of colonialism is the domination by the powerful over the weak. We today talk about neo-colonialism, hegemonism, pressure by great powers on smaller countries and of course about the last vestiges of colonialism in Africa, especially in South Africa, Namibia etc. People in the developed world do not understand how intensely the nonaligned movement feels about these remnants of colonialism and about racialism and apartheid.

The Delhi Declaration made clear these anti-colonial origins and background of the movement.

Another major development within the movement is its preoccupation with questions of economic development and economic justice and equality among nations. While politics still constitutes the soul of nonalignment, the major preoccupation of the movement today is with the economic chasm that divides the developed and the developing nations—the so-called North-South question. The movement has not taken up this question in a confrontational spirit—it is fully aware that the economic problems of the world, of the developed as well as the developing countries, cannot be solved without cooperation between the two. As the Delhi Declaration says, the recovery of the developed countries is dependent on economic development in the South and *vice versa.* That is the fact of interdependence in the modern world. The developed and affluent countries might find it annoying to be constantly asked to transfer resources and technology to the developing countries, but it is not merely the cry of the dispossessed and the poor at the doors of the fortunate rich. There is a severely realistic logic in this. When I was recently in San Francisco I read the speech of President Reagan there in which he said that forty percent of the exports of the United States went to the developing countries. That is a big chunk of American exports and connected with it is the question of employment in the United States. Unless there is a major thrust in economic development and in the improvement of living standards in the third world how can full economic recovery take place in the North? This North-South economic division is as dangerous as the political and military division in the world today. For it is actually in this vast region of the third world that we get all the major economic, social and political discontents of the world. And it is also in this region that all the markets of the future are. Therefore, when the nonaligned nations put so much stress on economic cooperation between the developed and the developing countries, on global negotiations for a new international economic order and on some well-conceived immediate steps for alleviating the urgent economic difficulties of the South, they are not talking in philanthropic or idealistic terms but in terms that are realistic for themselves as well as for the great developed countries of the world.

Another major theme of the conference in Delhi was cooperation within the nonalignment movement and the developing world. We do not just want to sit and ask for transfer of resources and technology from the developed world, and wait for it idly though we believe that it is vitally important to begin the process of such a transfer here and how. But we want to develop cooperation among ourselves in a programme of collective self-reliance. Taken as a whole the developing countries have a rich variety of resources, raw materials and talents; some are abundant in raw materials, some have scientific and technological talent, a few even a surplus of them. Therefore it is possible to work out programmes of collaboration amongst the developing countries in what we call collective self-reliance, while at the same time working for the larger objective of overcoming the disparity between the developed and the developing nations. Indeed in the future this incipient economic programme of collective self-reliance might turn out to be a major strategy adopted by the third world.

There are various other issues which are regional as well as global that agitate the minds of the nonaligned. These important issues have also been addressed at the

Delhi summit like the problems of the Middle East, Afghanistan, Kampuchea, Latin America, etc.

The approach was not to apportion blame between one group of countries or another, but to go to the roots of the problems and try to point the way to possible solutions. In regard to Central America the main emphasis in the Delhi declaration was on the root causes of the problem, *viz.* the traditional power structures in these countries, the economic systems prevailing in these countries, the domestic political oppression existing in these countries, etc. According to the analysis of the nonaligned all these problems have been aggravated by intervention by outside forces, and it would be easier to solve them without such outside interference.

On Afghanistan we are aware that there is considerable sentiment in this country. What is important is that it was possible for the nonaligned conference to come to a consensus formulation on this issue; a formulation that calls for a political settlement, involving withdrawal of foreign troops, the return of the refugees in honour and safety and an agreement or guarantee on non-intervention or non-interference from outside, all of which we believe will enable Afghanistan to safeguard its sovereignty, territorial integrity and its nonaligned status. The question has been asked why we do not specifically condemn the Soviet Union whose troops are present there. As far as Indian policy is concerned, we have stated publicly as well as privately in our diplomatic representations that foreign troops must be withdrawn; we have stated it in Delhi, in Moscow and elsewhere. Withdrawal of troops is a major element in a political settlement, but there are other elements also to such a settlement.

The United Nations is involved in a very serious search

for a solution through the representatives of the Secretary General. Pakistan is involved now actively in these U.N. sponsored contacts and talks. One important point is that Afghanistan as well as the Soviet Union have declared themselves to be in favour of a dialogue on this issue. We are convinced that there could be no settlement of this question except through peaceful negotiations. On the question of Kampuchea too, though there was a great deal of debate at the Delhi Summit, a consensus was arrived at spelling out the elements of a comprehensive political settlement.

In this context, I should like to draw attention to the method of consensus by which agreements are reached at nonaligned conferences. In the formation of such consensus, regional views of member countries play an important part, of course within the larger framework of the principles and priorities of the movement. Thus on the Middle-East the views of the Arabs will have a leading role to play, on African issues those of the African countries, and on Latin American questions those of the Latin American countries. This does not mean that the nonaligned movement is regionally fragmented or that a group of countries could impose its positions on the movement. As a matter of fact, if even a small number of countries refuse to acquiesce in a certain formulation, it can hold up a consensus being reached. But it has been experience that almost invariably they accept what emerges as the general consensus. There is an essential solidarity in the movement which impels all to go along with a broad consensus even while individual countries or groups of countries may have differences or reservations on certain formulations of the conference. This has been possible because of the historic origins and the current compulsions of the nonaligned movement. Anticolonialism, nationalistic aspirations, economic deprivation, desire for peace, fear of war-like situations breaking out into wars, and the feeling that in a world where the great powers throw their weight about it is necessary to stick together at least in a loose form, all these have made the nonaligned come together in a consensus on the major issues of our time in spite of differences among them on some questions.

The nonaligned consensus is not a monolithic stand. Nor is the nonaligned movement a bloc or an alliance. It is a group of independent countries following independent policies. One could say that there are as many nonaiigned foreign policies as there are nonaligned countries. But all of them adhere to certain ideas and principles of the movement and pursue certain goals and aspirations common to them. The aim of the nonaligned movement is not to crystallize itself into a new bloc, but to carry its ideas to the minds of people everywhere including the United States and the Soviet Union. Jawaharlal Nehru had conceived it as a movement of ideas. Indeed the nonaligned today derive some of their support and strength from responses of people within the blocs to their major ideas on world peace, disarmament and development. The Delhi Summit has given new articulation to these ideas. It has not only produced a consensus on them among the nonaligned but drawn the attention of the whole world to them.

IV

The United Nations in an Uncertain World

I have a habit of being lucky on U.N. Day. The first time I spoke at a United Nations Day was years ago when I was invited to do so by the lady who later became my wife. And our second daughter was born on U.N. Day. Thus whether I like it or not I am involved in the United Nations!

I should like to discuss with you the long perspective of history against which the United Nations Organization was born. Students of political science know how society evolved over the ages from very small groups and primitive societies to the global society of today. Small tribes gave way to larger groupings, and then in the eighteenth and nineteenth centuries modern states appeared; then came various groups of states and now we have blocs of states and large conglomerations of states. Today we have a global organization like the United Nations and almost a global society. That has been the march of history. And during this long march there have been tribal conflicts, group conflicts within societies, and after the formation of states in the modern sense, wars between states. We had dominant and

Address to the World Affairs Society of George Washington University on October 24, 1983.

ambitious individuals who strove to control and conquer the world impelled by a kind of dream of world unity in a very retrogressive sense. Then we have had alliances of states fighting against each other as in the First and Second World Wars. Today in the blocs aligned against each other we have something more than the old alliances. We have an ideological and strategic confrontation on a global scale, a kind of total, deathly embrace. With wisdom this can perhaps be turned into a friendly interlocking of nations in global interdependence. We notice that in history side by side with divisions and conflicts there was also a basic trend towards greater unity and cooperation. That is how the League of Nations was born after the First World War and the United Nations Organization after the more disastrous Second World War. That is where we stand today. The U.N. is the symbol of this marginal victory of world cooperation over world conflict.

Almost concurrently with power conflicts the world has seen ideological contests also; often they were parts of the same struggle. There have been various types of ideological conflict and religious wars, the Crusades between Christianity and Islam, the religious wars between Catholics and Protestants—the Thirty Years War—and the worldwide struggle of our own times between communism and capitalism. In the end we know that Christians and Muslims settled down to live together, more or less peacefully, and Protestants and Catholics accepted an amicable standstill between them. India never saw any religious wars of that kind, though we have had passing conflicts and bloodshed. By and large there was religious toleration in India. As a result of this experience we believed that communism and capitalism would also, after a spell of cold war, accept the inevitability of co-existing together, even though they might not like each other or there was clash of ideas and interests between them. This is the perspective of history against which we viewed the world and saw in the United Nations an institutional mechanism for blunting the edges of conflict and for working out a *modus vivendi* among nations.

Revolutionary developments in science and technology have had a dramatic impact on this process. Technology contributed to conflict and confrontation in the world by creating instruments of mass destruction; it also produced at the same time powerful instruments and opportunities for world cooperation. Hence we are living in a world of anxiety and uncertainty in which we do not know how the forces of technology would be used, whether to provide the progress and plenty that the best human minds have dreamed of, or to make more and more weapons in a mad arms race and send mankind to ultimate destruction. Therefore we are at a climacteric in human history when it has to be decided whether we choose the path of peace and cooperation or of self-annihilation. Only that, unlike in the past, we have to chalk out the path of peace not after a war but *before* going to war. Today we are in the tragic situation that if we do not avoid war we would not have the choice of building the edifice of peace at the end of the war, because the end of a nuclear war or a star war will be the virtual end of mankind.

So we have to make the choice before a war breaks out unlike in earlier times. Herein lies the significance of the U.N. The United Nations was born, if I may use a poetic phrase, from "the giant agony" of mankind. The U.N. charter, as you know, was created to save succeeding generations from the scourge of war, to work out friendly relations among nations and to achieve international cooperation in political, economic, scientific and cultural fields.

Whether one likes the U.N. or not, it is very clear that we need the United Nations. It exists in the subconscious, though not always in the minds, of nations—even the great ones—as a forum of last resort to go to. It is sad that during the last ten years or so the great powers have been trying to avoid the U.N. and work outside of it on some central issues. As the Secretary General said in his report to the thirty-eighth General Assembly, multilateral diplomacy is being looked down upon and the great powers are resorting to bilateral diplomacy or group diplomacy. Bilateral diplomacy is important and essential but to bypass the U.N. and other international institutions on critical world problems means that solutions are sought mainly in the interest of particular nations or groups of nations ignoring he interests of other nations and of the world as a whole.

For example on economic issues concerning North and South or on the role of multilateral banking institutions some developed nations have shown a preference for taking up questions outside the U.N. or dealing bilaterally with developing countries. Even when individual nations are generous and well-intentioned the result is the projection of the power of an advanced nation on a weak recipient of aid. When aid is funneled through international institutions like the World Bank or the International Monetary Fund the political and economic interests of the donor nations are actually not sacrificed but only softened by multilateral cooperation. That is the significance of the current controversy as to whether aid should be predominantly bilateral, or mainly channelled through international institutions, and whether Global Negotiations should be conducted within the United Nations or in other and more limited fora.

I am afraid that the advanced nations of both the East and the West operate under constraints and narrow considerations that are similar though their philosophical grounds may be dissimilar.

This approach deviates from the mainstream of international cooperation. This is unfortunately happening when objective facts point to the necessity and unavoidability of closer international cooperation. Even the richest countries want to prosper still further and to enjoy their prosperity in an atmosphere of peace and security. When the rest of the world is poor and hungry or going up in flames of conflict even the strongest of nations cannot be an island unto itself and enjoy the fruits of prosperity in splendid isolation. Hence the importance of the role of U.N. to preserve peace and to promote a more equitable distribution of world resources.

As I remarked earlier, upto the middle of the sixties or even upto the early seventies, the U.N. was utilized by nations for trying to solve major world problems. India herself played an important role in those days in the settlement of problems like the Korean and the Indochina wars and the Lebanese and the Congo problems. Later came the period of detente which provided the U.N. with a greater role. Some progress was made during this period in the fields of world economic development and disarmament. Detente then got a reversal creating almost a war-like situation around the world—a world which despite its nuclear bipolarity has seen a significant diffusion of political power. In a sense a sharply bipolar world was easier for the super powers to deal with from the point of view of their interests, though it posed great dangers of frontal confrontation.

Now we get a situation where even the super powers do

not have the capacity to control situations round the world. That is partly because of the development of nuclear weapons and partly because consciousness among people has risen even in the smallest and least developed countries. People do not want to be controlled from centers in Moscow or Washington. Conscious of their own distinctive cultures, environment, interests and priorities, they want to pursue policies according to their own genius and circumstances rather than being dictated to from the centers of the two power blocs. Notwithstanding their military and economic helplessness, they have developed a challenging sense of self-respect. This is what is being demonstrated by small countries and peoples in Asia, Africa, Latin America and Europe.

Though the instruments of power have become excessively potent and massively destructive, in practical terms it has become difficult to focus them on small countries on issues which annoy and give minor headaches to the great powers as in Nicaragua, Angola, Poland etc. Of course among great powers themselves the use of force and of the new weaponry has become even more difficult and dangerous. We have today what I call a kind of paralysis of power as a result of the sheer overdevelopment of power. The great powers have to think of other methods, political, economic and psychological methods to deal with these problems.

This has created a dilemma for those who wield power. With so much power in their hands, when a situation develops somewhere that is felt to be against their interests, may not be directly but in terms of the old domino theory, there is great temptation to reach out for these instruments of power and try them in a limited, calculated way instead of trying political and negotiating methods. It may be that sometimes one can get away with such exercises of power in an immediate sense. But the dangers inherent in them are obvious and the long-term effects on the international situation could well be disastrous.

The nonaligned nations have put forward the proposition that it is necessary to see the conflicts in the world, particularly in the third world, in historical, economic, social and political terms, to enquire how they arose and from where they derived their dynamism. More often than not the root causes are in the country or in the region concerned though outside forces would have exploited and accentuated them. Hence, the nonaligned stand to tackle these issues without outside intervention and by attending to the internal conditions that gave rise to them.

We have come to a stage in which great powers cannot be deterred by "deterrence," by creating a massive counterforce. The so-called balance of power through deterrence is a shifting perilous equilibrium. It ignores the unpredictability of technology and also the power of the human being, of public opinion. One feels sometimes that the only way we can today influence great power behaviour, be it in the West or East, is through public opinion organized in various ways. I would not rule out the importance of Gandhian philosophy and methods in all this. The United Nations Organization which is in a real sense the conscience of the world has its natural ally in the public opinion of the world. It is possible to have a closer concordance between the United Nations and world opinion. I do not say that herein lies the answer but the opinions and aspirations of people expressed in individual countries and within the U.N. itself can be a big force. In fact the U.N. has increasingly become a forum for the average nation while great powers are finding it more and more difficult to use it as their pliable instrument.

I should like to draw your attention to another development. You know how irritated some people are with the United Nations. They ask what business have these "banana republics" and "two-penny half-penny" countries to come and sit in that august assembly and out-vote the great ones of the earth? This is precisely what was asked almost in every country when the common man and the working class were fighting for the right to vote and their political rights. The aristocrats and the upper classes asked: "How can these poor and ignorant people determine the laws and policies of the country? Is it not ridiculous for a millionaire and a peasant or a worker in a factory to have the same vote, the same influence?" This question was asked in terms of the internal development of democracy in almost every country, including England. In the same way representatives of great powers tend to look down upon the smaller countries in the U.N., and ask how decisions affecting important world issues could be decided by the vote of the majority in the U.N. when there are great nations sitting there who have all the power, the arms and the money. In the perspective of history what we are witnessing is the beginning of a struggle for democracy in international relations.

The nonaligned movement is one of the staunchest protagonists of this struggle and supporters of the United Nations. During the Nonaligned Summit in New Delhi Prime Minister Mrs. Indira Gandhi proposed an informal meeting for informal discussions at the summit level among heads of State and Government on some of the major issues concerning the present world situation. This proposal was made not because Mrs. Gandhi thought that something remarkable would come out of such a meeting, but because she saw that world leaders have not been meeting one another and some of them were not even on talking terms with each other at a time when the world situation was edging towards the brink of disaster.

The meeting was held within the U.N. partly to suit the convenience of everyone and partly to emphasize the role of the United Nations. What the Secretary General of the U.N., Mr. Javier Perez de Cueller, wrote on this proposal in his report to the General Assembly is interesting. He wrote: "Let me here point to a source of real encouragement. It is perhaps best symbolized in the proposal of the Chairman of the Seventh Nonaligned Summit Conference, Prime Minister Indira Gandhi, that the United Nations should be strengthened by a meeting of Heads of State or Government to give a fresh collective look at some of the major problems of the world. At this critical time in human relations it is encouraging that the Nonaligned Movement has spoken as a protagonist of the multilateral approach and of the purposes and principles of the Charter."

This informal summit took place in spite of negative responses from some of the great powers. I had the opportunity of sitting in and listening to the discussions. There was nothing frightfully new in what was said nor was there any agreement or decisions coming out of it—nothing like that was intended or expected. What was important was that some 25 to 30 heads of state and govenment sat across a table in a small room and talked to each other as ordinary human beings though holding power and responsibility in their own countries. They voiced their views and also their differences on vital issues like peace, disarmament, development, global negotiations etc. It showed how world leaders could hold a friendly dialogue even on disputatious issues and come away with a little more understanding of one another's positions. It was the first time that such an informal discussion at the summit level took place inside the U.N. with the participation of the Secretary General and the President of the General Assembly. It was a precedent-setting event and a thoroughly informal and non-committal method of exchanging ideas which world leaders can have recourse to in critical situations in the future. And it was a method designed to lend support to the United Nations Organization which is the best world body that we have and the best that we can have in the circumstances of our times.

V
Interdependence and Development

The theme of this Conference—Global Inter-dependence and National Development—suggests both the com-
plementarities and the contradictions inherent in the relations among nations today. While the world has shrunk to
"a global village" and become increasingly inter-dependent,
forces have also been at work in the opposite direction
pulling towards disunity and discord. For us in India this
duality has been a perennial experience and the constant
endeavour in our history has been to find unity in diversity,
to reconcile the individual to the society, the locality to the
nation, and the nation to the world.

It is well-known that the Indian mind has been inward-
looking and preoccupied with the question of individual
perfection, the realization of the self and the salvation of the
soul. What is not so well-known is that Indians from ancient
days had thought of humanity as one family, a single nest,
and "the whole world of mortals as an inter-dependent
organism" as the Mahabharata put it. In modern times
Mahatma Gandhi turned the inwardness into a dynamic

*Keynote Address on March 25, 1982, at the 8th Annual Third World
Conference organized by Governors State University, Chicago.*

43

force by putting his individual mind and soul against the might of an empire through his method of nonviolent non-cooperation. While he was prepared to stand alone, he saw life as an ever-widening circle of relationships in which the individual must work, and if necessary, sacrifice for the family, the family for the village, the village for the nation, and the nation for the world. He once said: "My service of India includes the service of humanity. Isolated independence is not the goal of the world states. It is voluntary inter-dependence. The better mind of the world desires today not absolutely independent states, but a federation of inter-dependent states. The consummation of that event may be far-off."

This far-off vision was before India when she became independent and it was in the light of it that Jawaharlal Nehru declared that India proposed to pursue her national interests in the context of international cooperation. First of all, we needed peace around us in the world in order to enable us to concentrate upon the questions of social and economic development of a country that was emerging from colonial domination and a long period of arrested growth. Secondly, we did not want to be drawn into cold war conflicts and be forced to take sides in the military-cum-ideological struggle of the two blocs, which would have not only disturbed our peaceful environment but divided our own people. Thirdly, we wanted friendship and lines of communications kept open with all countries so that we could get cooperation and assistance from all possible sources for our economic development. Fourthly, for consolidating the unity of a country as vast, diverse and problem-ridden as India, it was necessary to lift the sights of the people to wider horizons beyond India and to cast their lot with the future of the world itself. And finally, looking from the vantage point of our historically evolved world-view we perceived that modern developments, particularly the consequences of scientific and technological progress, were beginning to translate the old concept of an inter-dependent world into a palpable and practical reality. Thus on the eve of our Independence Jawaharlal Nehru stated our credo as follows: "The world, in spite of its rivalries and hatreds and inner conflicts, moves inevitably towards closer cooperation and the building up of a world commonwealth. It is for this One World that free India will work, a world in which there is free cooperation of free peoples, and no class or group exploits another." It was out of this totality of considerations that the policy of nonalignment and peaceful co-existence emerged which steered India clear off cold-war alignments towards the objective of friendship with all nations and peace in the world.

If we were obsessed with the question of war and peace, especially with the issue of nuclear war, it was not the result of moralistic posturing or idealistic frothing, as made out by writers in the West, but because of our understanding of its impact on India's interests and aspirations, and on the future of mankind. Today it is impossible to discuss the question of global inter-dependence and national development without facing up to this over-riding nuclear issue. One touch of the threat of nuclear war, if I may appropriate a line from Shakespeare, is today "making the whole world kin." It was nearly 25 years ago that Jawaharlal Nehru declared that in this nuclear age the choice of mankind was between "co-existence or co-destruction." I cannot but recall a friendly debate that Nehru had with Chairman Mao Tse-tung in 1954 when he visited the People's Republic of China. Those were the perfervid days of the doctrine of the inevitability of war. Mao expounded that the invention of nuclear weapons had not changed the nature of war in any substantial sense, except in its scale, and that even though 200 or 250 million people would be killed in a nuclear war, millions will survive particularly in the villages of countries like China and India. Nehru, on the other hand, argued that nuclear weapons have changed the nature of war and that apart from the destruction it would cause to civilization as we know it, the effects of radiation would leave mankind virtually annihilated. It is fascinating that though Mao is no more and China has set aside this doctrine, the shades of it still haunt several unlikely places, and we now hear talk about the possibility of a nuclear war, and winnability in such a war.

Neither global inter-dependence nor national development is of any avail unless this mad career of nuclear-missile armaments is arrested and reversed. Behind this arms race is not merely arms but the concept of an irreconcilable conflict between two super powers and two blocs. This concept is totally contrary to that of global inter-dependence. The Indian approach has been that there is no conflict in the world that cannot be resolved through peaceful means and through mutual accommodation, and even if conflict is imposed on us, to wage it with the future of the peoples concerned and of mankind in mind and, in the words of Nehru, with "the hands of friendship never withdrawn." The idea of an everlasting enmity is alien to the human mind and heart. It was George Washington who in his farewell address advised the United States against the twin evils of excessive animosity and excessive attachment to particular nations. To me it sounds a little like the approach of nonalignment. Speaking in 1958 Jawaharlal Nehru said: "All history points out that friends and allies sometimes become enemies, and enemies become friends, and the history of even the last twelve years has shown us this. Why then persist in a policy that perpetuates these enmities?" After pointing out that even the bloodiest of wars must come to an end and then the parties would have to seek peace, Nehru asked, "Why wait for a war before we seek peace?" The question is agonizingly pertinent today, because, for mankind a nuclear war will be a terrible, terminal war, and therefore we will have to seek peace before the war comes in order to avoid it.

Here we come to the question of disarmament, development and world peace. Man has today at his disposal the knowledge and the power to open up the cornucopia which would enable us to abolish hunger, and poverty, to raise the cultural levels of people everywhere, and to alleviate the thousand ills that afflict mankind, if only we eschew the massive misdirection of our resources and the misapplication of the fruits of science and technology. Even a limited agreement on disarmament by the great powers would release funds for development not only of the third world countries but of people on the margins of poverty line in the advanced countries. The confrontationist policies of the great powers have also played a part in the burden of armaments that is being imposed on the developing countries themselves. Eighty per cent of the arms sales in the world today are estimated to be to countries in the third world most of whom can ill afford this diversion of their resources from developmental purposes. It may be asked, are not countries like India not indulging in heavy expenditure on armaments? This is unfortunately true, but to a large extent it is the result of a vicious chain reaction set in by the cold war strategies of the super powers in the region of the third world, and by the policy of the advanced countries to sell arms for gaining political influence and for sheer profit. Nevertheless I should like to point out that as far as India is concerned, while taking every precaution to possess adequate arms for our defence, we spend only 3.58% of our GNP on defence which is well below the world average and below what is spent by our neighbours in Asia. The concentration of our resources and efforts is predominantly on social and economic development. I must add that our nuclear programme and our space programme are also dedicated to peaceful and constructive uses as shown not only by our solemn policy statements but our abstention from manufacturing atomic weapons having mastered in 1974 technical capability to explode a nuclear device. We believe that progress towards disarmament by the great powers would lessen the armament burden on the developing countries and release funds for accelerating the development process in the third world. That would be a major contribution to national development as well as global inter-dependence and world peace.

This brings us directly to the other most important issue of our time, the problem of development of the third world and the relationship between North and South. Abraham Lincoln at a critical period in the history of the United States told the American people that a house divided against itself cannot stand and a nation half-free and half-slave shall not endure. I should like to say that an inter-dependent world cannot endure, one-third rolling in affluence and two-thirds wallowing in poverty. It is really a misnomer to call the developing countries the third world. As Prime Minister Mrs. Indira Gandhi once put it, there is only one world, and that is the one world in which we all live. The so-called third world is an integral part of the same world. If one looks at it in this way the North-South question can be seen as one of inter-dependence and cooperation rather than one of competition and confrontation. Mrs. Gandhi speaking for the developing countries said at the Cancun Summit: "We are not supplicants. Nor are we confrontationists. It is our experience that the interests of the developed and developing countries are so inter-twined that we can all survive in harmony only in conditions of true interdependence . . . we earnestly seek a global compact which will ensure the development of the poorer countries along with the prosperity of the developed nations, in circumstances of international peace and security." Viewed in this light there is no reason for the advanced nations to be afraid of global negotiations on the North-South question or of the efforts of the developing countries to work for collective self-reliance among themselves.

In February this year representatives of 44 developing nations gathered together at New Delhi to consult with one another as to how they could cooperate among themselves and promote the North-South dialogue. Mrs. Gandhi set the tone for this conference when she said in her inaugural address that: "Inter-dependence is the rationale of the dialogue and cooperation between North and South," and that economic progress in the developing countries can rejuvenate the stagnating economies of the developed world. The concept of collective self-reliance in the third world is neither puerile idealism nor a challenge to the developed nations. It is an attempt to do whatever they can by themselves and to promote cooperation with the North. The Brandt Report had tried to show how the North and South are interdependent and how the jobs and the daily lives of people in the North are interlocked with the interests of poorer communities at the other end of the world. There are nearly 3.25 billion people inhabiting the developing countries. According to Robert McNamara these are the fastest growing markets in the world and hundreds of thousands of jobs in the United States depended on improvement in the plight of the people in these regions. Quite apart from this enlightened argument of inter-dependence, it has also to be considered in a realistic manner whether the developed world can flourish in-definitely as islands of prosperity in a surging sea of deprived and discontented humanity.

It has often been pointed out that while countries of the North are themselves undergoing severe economic dif-ficulties how they could be expected to incur undue sacrifices for aiding people in other parts of the world. The economic problems of the North are real and these must be taken into full account in any scheme of North-South dialogue. But as has been argued earlier aid for devel-opment in the South is one of the long-term methods of overcoming the problems of unemployment and slow growth rates in the North. Perhaps it must also be pointed out that the economic hardships of people of the advanced countries fall in a category somewhat different from those of the developing countries where the struggle is for the basic necessities and amenities of life. An aristocratic character in Leo Tolstoy's novel "War and Peace," who went to the battle front in the war against Napoleon, and who had to sleep on the ground together with the common soldiers, mused that the discomfort a man in his bed of roses suffered because of a crumpled petal was just as much as what he suffered lying on the hard, damp ground. This may be psychologically true, certainly in the aristocratic scale of values. But to go without a second car, or an MX or SS-20 missile is perhaps not as agonizing and degrading as to go without a second meal or a primary school or a dispensary.

The role of private enterprise in relation to official

development assistance and aid through multilateral financial institutions has become a matter of policy differences
today. As far as the developing countries are concerned they
believe that aid and cooperation must flow through all these
three channels. Private enterprises, particularly the multinationals, have become major engines for investment and
transfer of technology in the world today. It has been
estimated that direct investments by multinationals in the
world have reached the level of $500 billion. That they have
a part to play in third world development is undeniable. But
unlike in the hey-day of capitalism when risks were taken
almost recklessly, resulting in the building up of great
fortunes and even Empires, private enterprise today seeks
cast-iron guarantees and the shelter and support of governments before they go into foreign countries especially
into the third world countries. And there are also areas of
development in which they are not likely to show interest.

This is one of the reasons why official development aid
and assistance through international institutions like the
World Bank and I.M.F. are crucial for third world
development. While I say this I must make it clear that in
my country conditions have emerged, largely due to the
stage of economic development that we have now reached,
for foreign private enterprise to invest and involve themselves in a wide variety of economic projects. India is not
only a vast potential market but a place for secure
investment by foreign companies. However, aid through
multi-lateral institutions and official channels is indispensable for the developing countries for their development
and for promoting larger cooperative relations with the
countries of the North.

Official development aid has not only practical but
profoundly symbolic significance in the sense of the

commitment of the North to the development of the South and to the establishment of a better equation between the two. One of the disappointing trends of the times has been the diminution of this category of assistance. Even more disturbing is the threatened reduction in aid through IDA, the soft-loan affiliate of the World Bank. All these mark retrograde steps on the path of global inter-dependence. It was in the context of the American War of Independence that the greatest and the most far-seeing political philosopher of conservatism, Edmund Burke, told the British Parliament that "a great Empire and narrow minds go ill together." I think Edmund Burke would have told the advanced nations of today that great affluence and a narrow world vision go ill together.

That the affluent and the advanced have responsibilities to the developing nations is not the argument of the beggar for charity. Indeed the scientific-technological advances and the present prosperity in Europe and America have not come about suddenly or entirely indigenously. They have been the product of long interaction among nations over many centuries—products, if I may put it irreverently, of the harlotry of international exchange, cooperation and exploitation. It is known that the European Renaissance was impelled by knowledge and ideas that travelled from the East to the West through the Arab lands, and my own country, India, had contributed some of the basic concepts in mathematics and geometry without which the scientific-industrial revolution would have been inconceivable. And the economic development of the United States owes much to the capital and technology first brought and then dramatically expanded in this New World. Thus it ought to be remembered that the advanced knowledge and the affluence of the North is the outcome of a prolonged historical process of inter-change and inter-dependence among peoples and nations. And this process is not likely to stop where it is today, unless those who have attained this power and wealth turn to the final folly of self-annihilation.

While the problems of the Third World are those of food, energy, capital, finance and trade, behind these lie the even more basic questions of educational, cultural, scientific and technological progress. Unless these basic questions are tackled, the gap between the developed and the developing countries will become in the future wider and unbridgeable. Hence the relevance of the question of transfer of technology and the development of education and knowledge in the third world. The efforts of the developing countries to advance in the higher realms of science and technology, like nuclear and space science, are sometimes looked upon with amusement and suspicion. It is asked why a poor country like India should indulge in nuclear research and set up nuclear reactors, or try to launch space satellites, or send expeditions to the Antarctic and be concerned with the seabed and the laws of the sea and the outer space. The answer is that in order to deal successfully with the colossal elementary needs of our people, while working and sweating on our soil and in our factories, we have got simultaneously to try to reach out to the stars and into the depths of the oceans. The present tendency is for nations that are technologically advanced and militarily strong to corner what they want often disregarding the rights of others and the interests of humanity as a whole. If the disparity in scientific-technological know-how and in the application of it to the undiscovered and unexploited regions of the universe persists and widens, we would be facing a situation in the future when the developing countries might find themselves relatively even less developed than today, and when a few advanced nations might well emerge as the new technological overlords of the world.

The progress of the third world is, therefore, an indispensable factor for global inter-dependence and for a healthy balance in the world order. The struggle of the developing nations for a fair share in wealth, resources and technology, for better living conditions for the millions of people who live there, for balanced and rapid development, and for acquiring individual and collective self-reliance to the maximum extent possible, is thus of far-reaching significance.

On her part India has right from the beginning of her independence adopted a strategy for development geared to these objectives, but not in an isolationist or autarchic manner, but by remaining in the main-stream of international cooperation.

The attainment of basic self-sufficiency in food production is evidence of the priority we gave to the needs of our people in our developmental strategy. I must here acknowledge the contributions made by the United States to our green revolution in India. We have, however, not neglected our industrial progress, and even though India today is a predominantly agricultural country and shall remain so in the future, it is ranked as the tenth industrialised nation in the world. Further, notwithstanding the fact that we have yet to catch up with the rest of the world in general educational progress, we have even today the third largest pool of scientific and technical personnel in the world. The industrial and technological infra-structure built up in our country is of such diversity, sophistication and magnitude that the prospects are bright for further rapid advance in industrialisation and modernisation. In spite of this achievement the problems of development, of equitable distribution, and of fulfilling the needs and aspirations of our people remain gigantic tasks yet to be accomplished. The growth of population is an enormous problem in itself. It has, however, not been understood that during the last one decade we have managed to slow down the rate of population growth despite a radical decline in the death rate and downward trend in infant mortality. In some parts of the country like the State of Kerala, the family planning programme has been so successful that the growth rate has come down to 1.8%. Our experience in family planning has shown that population control is not the result of a special or separate effort, but of development itself, especially of advance in the education of women. Here, I should like to say that the rising status of women in India is one of the important factors contributing to social, economic and cultural development in our country and it has facilitated our cooperation with the developing and developed countries of the world.

One of the lessons we have learnt from our developmental experience is that maximum degree of self-reliance in agriculture, industry and science and technology has to be acquired if we are to maintain our independence and independent policies, and cooperate with the advanced nations on terms that are not entirely unequal. We believe that the developing nations by concerting their policies and programmes on basic issues of common interest and by building up collective self-reliance could generate sufficient strength and confidence for dealing with the powerful and rich advanced nations. India has tried her best to share the industrial and technological know-how it has acquired with other developing nations, and we have today some significant collaboration projects in various countries of Asia, the Middle-East and Africa. We believe that it is by beginning with a network of cooperation in our region and in the third world that we can negotiate credibly with the developed countries for meaningful cooperation. I must add here that we believe very strongly that in all this the United Nations Organization and its agencies have a crucial role to play.

One important feature of India's development strategy is that it has been conceived in democratic terms and carried out within the framework of democracy. The application of the democratic method to social and economic development of such massive proportions is to my mind a unique experiment in development. The economic successes of the capitalist system were achieved in Europe before the advent of full democracy, while the colossal social and economic changes brought about in the USSR, China and other socialist countries were under the aegis of totalitarian political system. At first it was believed that to develop India democratically would be choosing the slowest road to progress. But as it has now turned out that progress, though gradual and peaceful, has been steady, substantial and enduring.

One question is asked of India and other developing countries. Are they embarking upon a mere mechanistic process of accumulating and accelerating material production and imitating the pattern followed by the developed countries of today? Or are they adapting industrialisation and science and technology to their specific needs and trying to fit them into their indigenous social-cultural milieu. Our endeavour in India has not been blind imitation. We have tried to create a mixed economy combining elements of socialism with some of the dynamic incentives of private enterprise. I must, however, emphasise that in the Indian economic system, while the heavy industries and undertakings of public interest are in the public sector, the entire agricultural and small and medium scale industries are in the private sector. It was necessary in our situation, as in most developing countries, to bring about a balance in our strategy between production and growth and the compulsions of social justice.

There is one more aspect of the Indian development which deserves emphasis. Being an old society and ancient civilisation, while speeding up material progress we also maintain our cultural traditions and values which we believe will have a softening as well an enriching effect on development; our endeavour is to add a cultural dimension to our industrial and technological advancement while at the same time rejecting traditions and values which have become outmoded and which impede progress. As the developmental process in India has moved within a complicated social-cultural system and within a peaceful democratic framework, there has been no high drama attached to this experiment as in the case of changes brought about by violent upheavals in some other societies; but the results have been considerable and have given hope to over the one-sixth of mankind inhabiting our country, and provided a basis for meaningful cooperation with the developing as well as the developed countries for fashioning a new and just international order.

VI

Asia—An Indian Perspective

India's perspective on Asia was fashioned by two sets of factors, one domestic and the other international, both connected with each other in an almost organic manner. Over centuries India had evolved as a complex society and a composite culture, receiving and assimilating streams of thought, ideas and life-styles from outside, and issuing forth impulses and influences that left lasting imprints upon the religious, philosophical and cultural life of people almost in every part of Asia. In modern times the advent of colonialism—the multi-headed colonialism of European powers—snapped these historical links among Asian countries making them colonies ruled in isolation by particular European powers. But this common subjection imposed on Asia by Western colonialism also aroused a common nationalism that eventually convulsed the whole of Asia and Africa culminating in the liberation of one Asian-African nation after another.

India was the first nation that achieved its independence, after a prolonged and peaceful struggle, opening the

Keynote speech at the Tenth Annual meeting of the Mid-Atlantic Region of the Association for Asian Studies on October 16, 1981 held at the University of Maryland.

sluicegates of national liberation, and at the same time providing a method of reconciliation and co-operative relationship on the basis of freedom and equality with the erstwhile colonial masters. In our approach to Asia was involved the acceptance of the multiplicity of religious, philosophical, political and social beliefs and patterns that characterized the world of India itself, and also our view of the larger world as a place where different nations, big and small, with different social and political systems and even antagonistic doctrines and ideologies, could flourish and even compete with each other within a framework of peaceful co-existence.

India was acutely aware of the rivalries and conflicts that had arisen in this world, but we believed that in the new and dangerous age of nuclear weapons and missiles, efforts at peaceful co-existence were not only necessary but inevitable for the survival of human civilization and mankind itself. India looked upon herself and the rest of emergent Asia as a force for peace, and not as playthings and instruments of power-politics in the hands of great powers that had now become colossal super powers or closely-knit and cold-war oriented alliance systems dividing the world into two warring camps. We saw in this situation the necessity as well as an opportunity to try to direct resurgent Asia along a third path, that of nonalignment and peaceful co-existence. We were convinced that if we followed the traditional path of European rivalries and balance of power politics and joined with the new cold war alliance systems, our newly-won freedom and independence would be endangered, and our newly-awakened dreams of development and progress for our people reduced probably to mere dust and ashes.

On September 7, 1946 almost a year before our

Independence, Jawaharlal Nehru in a famous broadcast speech, after sending the greetings of new India and offering friendship and co-operation to Great Britain, United States and the Soviet Union, said as follows about Asia: "We are of Asia, and the peoples of Asia are nearer and closer to us than others. India is so situated that she is the pivot of Western, Southern and Southeast Asia. In the past, her culture flowed to all these countries and they came to her in many ways. Those contacts are being renewed and the future is bound to see a closer union between India and Southeast Asia on the one side, and Afghanistan, Iran, and the Arab world on the other. To the furtherance of that close association of free countries we must devote ourselves."

Even though India was partitioned since Nehru made this statement and her position as the pivot of Western and Southern Asia has somewhat diminished as a result of it and also as a result of the rise of China and Japan as great powers and of ASEAN as a new grouping in Southeast Aisa, India still occupies, in a potentially substantial sense, such a position on account of her size, strategic location, her population, industrial development, agricultural success, scientific and technological advance, the size and competence of her armed forces, and the as yet untapped human and material resources at her disposal. At the same time it must be understood that India is not one of those countries driven by a will to power and glory placing acquisition of power and prestige in the region or in the world as its first priority. She is in a real sense the gentle giant mainly concerned with the safeguarding of her basic interests and the safeguarding of peace around her which she sees as the precondition for the solution of the immense problems at home and for the fulfilment of her ultimate destiny in the world.

In the beginning Jawaharlal Nehru had entertained a vague dream of Asian cooperation in the form of an Asian Federation or some such loosely-knit Asian organization. He believed that the whole outlook and spirit of Asia was peaceful and "the emergence of Asia in world affairs will be a powerful influence for world peace." However, as the harsh realities of Asian politics and the impact of world rivalries on Asia developed, he realized that it was not a practical proposition and that all that could be achieved was cooperation among the nations of Asia on issues that were of common concern for them. The Asian Relations Conference held in Delhi in 1947 heralded to the world the emergence of Asia as a new factor in world politics; the Conference on Indonesia that Nehru called in New Delhi in 1949 exercised crucial influence on the United Nations in its consideration of the Indonesian question, and the Colombo Conference of the five Asian powers, India, Pakistan, Burma, Indonesia and Ceylon, made an impact on the 1954 Geneva Conference on Indo-China. And finally, the Bandung Conference of 1955 registered the high-water mark of Asian cooperation embracing almost all the newly independent nations of the time in Asia as well as Africa.

These early gatherings of Asian nations cannot be described as conferences of nonaligned nations though the thread of nonalignment ran through them, often clashing with the forces of alignment that were emerging in Asia then. This clash was clear both at Colombo and Bandung with Pakistan standing on the edge of entry into Wetsern sponsored military pacts and acting almost as the leader of the aligned faction. Cutting across the new East-West cold war concept, Nehru with the support of U. Nu of Burma and Soekarno of Indonesia, succeeded both at Colombo and Bandung to put across the independent position in international affairs adopted by the new nations of Asia. In the communique of the Colombo Conference he managed to get a formulation which was essentially nonaligned and which opposed intervention of outside powers in Asia. The five Prime Ministers declared their "unshakable determination to resist interference in the affairs of their country by external communist, anti-communist and other agencies" and also declared that "such interference threatened the sovereignty, security and political independence of their respective States and the right of each country to develop and progress in accordance with the conceptions and desires of its own people."

It was the same independent, nonaligned stand that emerged, although in a somewhat compromised form, from the Bandung Conference. Bandung marked the sharpest yet contest between the aligned and nonaligned view-point in Asia, and nonalignment came out of it with sharper focus expressing itself in a more challenging language. The strategy of Nehru at the Conference was first of all to attain the maximum possible agreement upon an independent stand by Asian-African nations in world affairs, and secondly in a two-pronged move to wean away Asian-African countries from a Western dominated alliance system that was trying to draw them into it and at the same time to bring out the People's Republic of China into the Asian-African fold and into the world as a whole in order to enable it to loosen itself from the control of the Soveit alliance system. Both of these objectives did not materialize fully, partly because of the lack of understanding on the part of the Western powers of the nature of Asian nationalism, the nature of the Chinese revolution and the peculiar character of the relationship that marked Sino-Soviet relationship.

In his concluding speech at Bandung Nehru declared: "If I join any of the big groups, I lose my identity." He then asked: "Are we the countries of Asia and Africa devoid of any positive position except being pro-communist or anti-communist?" and he pleaded: "Let us not align ourselves as independent nations of Asia and Africa, but take a line of our own. I do not say that it should be a single line." Nehru also asked: "If all the world were divided up between these two big blocs what would be the result? The inevitable result would be war. Therefore, every step that takes place in reducing that area in the world which may be called the 'unaligned area' is a dangerous step that leads to war." That was the perspective of India on Asia and the world at a critical point in Asian and world history.

Though the Indian view did not fully prevail at Bandung, it did come out as the dominant view, a view that is valid even today in safeguarding the independence of Asian nations and in preserving peace not only in Asia, but in the world as a whole. Two military pacts that emerged in Asia in contradiction to the nonaligned path advocated by India, viz. the SEATO and the Baghdad Pact have now receded into the limbo of history though their ghosts still raise their heads in nebulous forms like "strategic consensus" or "strategic relationship" helmeted by sophisticated military technology.

The extraordinary stress that India put on independent policies, on nonalignment and co-existence had reasons much deeper than political and diplomatic. We were and are opposed to totalitarian ideologies and political systems of one kind or another, and we are passionately devoted to the principles and processes of democracy. But we have been persuaded from the very outset of our independence that extremist totalitarian ideologies can be effectively combatted not by arms and by cold war crusades but by ideas, policies and programmes in the social, political, economic and psychological realms. In this struggle it is also important that we should act independently and put ourselves at the crest of the nationalist sentiments and aspirations of our people and not rely upon foreign support and foreign arms, and appear to act on behalf of external agencies.

If India has today established itself as a democracy, keeping extremist anti-democratic parties within the limits of political ineffectiveness, it is because our leadership has always put themselves in tune with the nationalistic aspirations of our people and refused to align ourselves with one side or other in the international crusade of our times. While adopting this fundamental strategy we also have not ignored the fact that when the freedom and liberty of our people are threatened by subversion and when law and order are challenged, and when people take the law into their hands and indulge in violence, the State has the duty to summon all the forces at its command to protect the democratic system. It is in this light of our experience that we have looked upon the Asian scene where social, economic and political conditions are not far different from our own, though differences exist and therefore variations of methods may be called for.

This brings us nearer home to Indian perspective on our own neighbourhood, South Asia itself, because we cannot have an Asian perspective or a valid world perspective without a credible and coherent view of our own neighbourship. In this respect Pakistan occupies pride of place. The partition of India was brought about through mutual agreement. It was the hope of India that after partition the two States would live together in peace and co-operation with each other. In one of his early speeches after partition Jawaharlal Nehru spelt out his vision in this way: "I believe," he said, "that for a variety of reasons, it is inevitable that India and Pakistan would draw closer to one another, or else they will come into conflict. There is no middle way, for we have known each other too long to be indifferent neighbours. I believe, indeed, that in the present context of the world, India must develop a closer union with many other neighbouring countries. But all this does not mean any desire to strangle or to compel Pakistan. Compulsion there can never be, and an attempt to disrupt Pakistan would recoil to India's disadvantage. If we had wanted to break Pakistan, why did we agree to the partition? It was easier to prevent it then than to try to do so now after all that has happened. There is no going back in history. As a matter of fact, it is to India's advantage that Pakistan should be a secure and prosperous State with which we can develop close and friendly relations. If today by any chance I were offered reunion of India and Pakistan, I would decline it for obvious reasons. I do not want to carry the burden of Pakistan's great problems. I have enough of my own. Any closer association must come out of a normal process, and in a friendly way."

Thus it was never the idea of India and of Indian leadership to weaken Pakistan but to see it as a stable state in normal friendly relations with India. That vision remains with us, even though we have fought three wars, and even though at this very moment, ignoring the lessons of history, more sophisticated arms and equipment are contemplated to be supplied to Pakistan, which would delay and make it more difficult the realization of Indo-Pakistan friendship and co-operation. We have always believed that the intrusion of outside powers, and the supply of sophisticated arms and equipment under formal military pacts or under informal strategic consensus would, far from strengthening Pakistan or contributing to Indo-Pakistan amelioration of relations or safe-guarding the stability and security of the region, would have results that are opposite and upsetting.

The vision of friendly and co-operative relations with Pakistan that Jawaharlal Nehru had entertained has been the guiding objective of Indian policy in the subcontinent. It was that vision which was embodied in the Simla Agreement of 1972 which solemnly declared that: "The Government of India and the Government of Pakistan are resolved that the two countries put an end to the conflict and confrontation that have hitherto marred their relations and work for the promotion of friendly and harmonious relationship and the establishment of durable peace in the sub-continent," and which also undertook to "settle their differences by peaceful means through bilateral negotiations or by any other peaceful means mutually agreed upon between them." Prime Minister Mrs. Gandhi has reiterated India's commitment to the Simla Agreement; so has the leadership of Pakistan, and it is by observing and extending the provisions and the spirit of this solemn pact that the two great neighbours in the sub-continent can improve their relations and help create a system of good neighbourliness in the South Asian region. It is in this spirit and with this vision in view that India has sought to regulate its relations with the other important sovereign states in the sub-continent viz., Bangladesh, Nepal and Bhutan. We believe that such a good neighbourly sub-continental system will emerge only if the region is fully insulated from the cold war politics and the power games of the great powers while remaining in the mainstream of international co-operation.

In a sense India in Asia has a Janus-faced geo-political

position facing West Asia on one side and Southeast Asia on the other, and in addition facing towards the north both China and Soviet Asia. With West Asia or the Middle East as it is called here, India has continued to the present day its age-old close cultural, economic and political ties. We had always believed that whether it is in the region of the Persian Gulf or the Arab world as a whole, nonalignment was the best foreign policy available for safeguarding the independence and security of the region. Given the facts of nationalism in this vast region, the cultural pride and the national self-respect of the peoples of the region and their aspirations for independence and stability, nonalignment is a natural and inevitable choice for these countries and any introduction of foreign forces or setting up of military bases or any massive induction of foreign military aid, is likely to be considered as intervention from outside and would arouse eventually the nationalist sentiments of the people against their own governments and the foreign powers concerned irrespective of their ideological complexion.

In regard to the situation in Afghanistan which impinges upon West Asia as well as South Asia, India's position has been very clear viz. all foreign troops must withdraw, Soviet troops, and any other foreign military personnel operating in that country, and that the country must be guaranteed against all manner of external intervention. We are convinced that the Afghanistan problem can be solved through political and diplomatic methods through talks and negotiations among the parties concerned, and not through military presence, armed interference and cold war strategies. Since the end of the Second World War, all the major conflict-situations in the world were finally settled by resort to negotiations, often between parties which did not diplomatically recognize one another, but which nevertheless sat at the conference table and talked to one another producing, however gradually and painfully, political settlements ending armed conflicts. India's stand on Afghanistan is calculated to help the emergence of a negotiated settlement while maintaining our basic position with regard to the necessity and inevitability of the withdrawal of foreign troops from that freedom-loving country.

With Southeast Asia India's relations have been even closer. There are four major power factors in this vital region viz. the three Asian giants—China, Japan and India—and the ASEAN group. In the historical past China and India had reached out to this region and had managed to co-exist without coming into conflict with each other. Immediately before and during World War II Japan had played an aggressive role in this region; but today Japan is a major force for peace and has involved itself in Southeast Asia in a constructive and co-operative way. It has been the Indian view that any new dispensation in Asia must ensure the independence and sovereignty of the nations of Southeast Asia and underwrite their nonalignment or neutrality as the case may be. There is of course a fifth major factor in the region—the super powers and the great powers. Even at the Bandung Conference there was no move on the part of the Asian nations to oust the influence of outside powers altogether from Asia or to exclude co-operation with them. What was opposed at Bandung was their colonial or colonial-like presence and their military intrusions. Indian position has remained the same, be it in South East Asia or in Asia as a whole or in the immense Indian Ocean that bounds it geographically and strategically. It is important that while maintaining their legitimate co-operative and peaceable interests in the region, the super powers must not bring into it their rivalries and conflicts and their domineering military presence. This applies to the great Asian powers themselves.

In 1954 Jawaharlal Nehru had made a proposal, in the context of a settlement in Indo-China, for "a convention of non-intervention" to which the United States, the Soviet Union, Britain, France and China were to be the main signatories. Nehru had envisaged that other states could be invited to adhere to this "convention of non-intervention" and that in due course it could be extended beyond Indo-China to the region as a whole. What is significant is that Asian powers also were to be parties to this convention at the centre of which was the concept of non-intervention. In the middle 60's Prime Minister Mrs. Gandhi made a proposal for a General Convention to be signed by Asian powers providing for mutual respect and guarantees for the independence, sovereignty and territorial integrity of the countries of the region and the neutrality or nonalignment of those countries which wished to remain neutral or nonaligned. At the core of the Indian view of a concord in Asia is co-existence and co-operation among the Asian powers and effective respect for the sovereignty and independence of the countries of Southeast Asia and other countries. All this is envisaged within the larger framework of international co-operation and also friendship with the super powers and great powers but without their domineering presence or their dividing and contending intrusions in the region.

VII
Islam in India

This year India is celebrating the 1500th anniversary of
the Hijra marking the beginning of the Islamic era.
Inaugurating the celebrations, Prime Minister Mrs. Indira
Gandhi said: "We, in India, celebrate this anniversary with
grateful awareness of the rich and varied contribution that
Islam has made to the evolution of our composite civilization."

To mark the occasion, a magnificent exhibition was
mounted at the National Museum in Delhi on the "Islamic
Heritage of India." It displayed a rare collection of Islamic
art ranging from resplendent swords of sultans and emperors to jewelled goblets and plates, storeyed gold and
silver coins, priceless manuscripts and exquisite miniature
paintings. The contribution of Islam to India was, however,
much too vast and varied to be conveyed adequately
through an exhibition. For Islam was one of the major
forces that shaped, over a thousand years, the cultural,
social, economic and political history of India, and which,
while remaining distinct, was woven into the fabric of

*Address at the Tenth Annual Conference on South Asia held at the
University of Wisconsin, Madison on November 7, 1981.*

Indian life and culture.

Jawaharlal Nehru once likened India to "some ancient palimpsest on which layer after layer of thought and reverie had been inscribed, and yet no succeeding layer had completely hidden or erased what had been written previously." In this Indian palimpsest the Islamic layer is one of the latest and clearest. Islam in its triumphant march from the sands of Arabia to the shores of the Atlantic in the West and to the islands of the Pacific in the east, has overcome and transformed some of the ancient civilizations of the world like those of Egypt and Persia. But as an historian put it: "India is the one exception where neither Islam has been overpowered by India, nor has India been absorbed into the Islamic mould."*

The story of Islam in India has not been one of a new militant force overwhelming an old civilization nor of the latter swallowing and digesting the former. It has been what one might call, a prolonged process of mutual accommodation and adjustment interspersed with stormy periods of antagonism and conflict.

The genius of India has often been said to be a capacity to absorb and assimilate new ideas and values as an ocean would absorb the waters of the rivers that flow into it. It has been also argued that Islam formed an exception to this, introducing, for the first time, "into the heart of India, a new unassimilable interpretation of the meaning and end of life." To my mind both these views are at once incomplete and exaggerated. There is no doubt that the new religion and the political force represented by Islam introduced different and disturbing concepts and codes of conduct and caused convulsions in Indian society and politics. At the same time

Cultural Heritage of India. Vol. IV. Page 579. Ramakrishna Mission Institute of Culture, Calcutta.

there had emerged rather early in the historic meeting of the Hindu and Islamic civilizations a process of cultural interpenetration and of mutual understanding and accommodation. The partition of India was a spectacular departure from this process of historical evolution. However, if one delves deeper into facts, and peeps a little ahead into the future, it would be seen that forces at work in favour of co-existence and cooperation are stronger, in the long run, than those that seek to retard and frustrate it.

Partition did not result in gathering together separately into two sovereign states all the Hindus and Muslims of the subcontinent. On the contrary, there are today 80 million Muslims living in India as Indian citizens as against almost the same number of Muslims living in Pakistan. India is actually the third largest Islamic nation in the world. Thus even though a political separation has taken place into India and Pakistan, Hindus and Muslims still live together in India, involved in each other and sharing a common destiny.

The separation of Bangladesh from Pakistan as a sovereign independent state has shown that the main point of departure in the sub-continent was not religion, but politics and economics. There are areas of differences as well as areas of affinity and cooperation in the sub-continent that fall outside the vortex of religion and that could be more compelling than the call of religion.

The Indian Muslim, while he retains his distinctiveness as a Muslim and is aware of his link with the wider world of Islam, is at the same time an Indian and is distinct from Muslims in other parts of the world. This is due to the prolonged and particular impact of the environment of India on him just as geographical, historical and cultural factors have influenced and moulded Muslims living in several other countries of the world today. As regards India and Pakistan, notwithstanding many serious differences, the peoples of the two countries react to each other as people more vividly and effortlessly and with what one might call an inner shock of recognition than perhaps any other two peoples in the world.

I have pointed out these basic affinities not for the purpose of minimising the fact of the differences or the problems of living together, but to emphasize what has often been ignored viz., that Hindus and Muslims have been and are living peacefully together in India and that compulsions of co-existence and co-operation between India and Pakistan are far more powerful than the forces that work in the opposite direction.

Let me go back to the old theme of the Indian genius for absorbing and assimilating races, cultures and ideas that have historically come from outside or arisen within India itself like Buddhism. Perhaps India has done more of this sort of mixing and mingling and melting, in its long history, than any other country. But in fact, India has been more of a mosaic than a melting pot, more an example of co-existence than of assimilation, more an experiment of unity in diversity than an extinguishing of diversities in order to create a new unity. It is this genius of India that Jawaharlal Nehru had in mind when he wrote: "Some kind of a dream of unity has occupied the mind of India since the dawn of civilization. That unity was not conceived as something imposed upon from outside, a standardization of externals or even of beliefs. It was something deeper and, within its fold, the widest of tolerance of belief and custom was practised, and every variety acknowledged and even encouraged." At some of the high watermarks of Indian history, be it under Asoka or Akbar or Nehru, it was this transcendental aspect of Indian culture that was evoked as the foundation of the subtle and complex structure of a unity in diversity, of a unity through tolerance and a sense of common destiny. Today even in the thick of the party politics of democracy, it is this same concept that has emerged. Mr. Syed Shahabuddin, an opposition member of the Indian Parliament and a distinguisehd Muslim has written as follows: "The Muslim mind, perplexed and bewildered by the pulls and pressures and the march of circumstances, is beginning to realize, on the one hand, the futility of confrontation as strongly as the repugnance of assimilation, on the other. But it is psychologically ready for integration, for a *modus vivendi,* in peace and honour, and for participation in the great cause of building a new India.* Mr. Shahabuddin also asserted that since the liberation of Bangladesh, Muslim India has realized that it was "India which was the repository of all that was of a permanent nature in the Islamic heritage of the sub-continent." I should not wish to make any claim for my country, but I believe that Muslims have a vital stake in India and the future of the Muslims and of the Hindus of India, indeed of the whole sub-continent, lies in co-existence and cooperation among the communities as well as the sovereign states constituting this region.

The onus for promoting this historic destiny does not fall on the shoulders of any one community only. Of course, the leadership in India of the majority community is acutely aware of their responsibility. In 1947 even when the wounds of partition were still raw, Jawaharlal Nehru wrote: "We have a Muslim minority who are so large in numbers that they cannot, even if they want to, go anywhere else. They

Illustrated Weekly of India, November 23, 1980.

have got to live in India. That is a basic fact about which there can be no argument. Whatever the provocation from Pakistan. . . . we have got to deal with this minority in a civilized manner. We must give them security and the rights of the citizens in a democratic state. If we fail to do so, we shall have a festering sore, which will eventually poison the whole body-politic and probably destroy it." Thus for both Hindus and Muslims as well as for other religionists in India co-existence and cooperation with one another remain the inescapable predicament. In fact that has been the normal situation throughout our long history, though we have had unhappy periods when the dream of unity was rudely broken and turned into nightmare.

Nearly two thousand years ago the Jews came to India. Though a tiny community, they have survived over the centuries preserving their religion, customs, manners and rituals, in short their identity, in a vast sea of Hindu humanity. Christianity came to India in the first century A.D. It spread through conversions, and today there are 14 million Christians in our country. Never losing its religious identity and authenticity, Christianity flourished, interacting with and absorbing some of the customs and manners and the culture of the Hindus. Even the small Zoroastrian community of Parsis have held their own in India and maintained their distinctive religious and social identity. Of course, the great non-Hindu religions of Buddhism, Jainism and Sikhism arose from the cultural matrix of India itself and the history of their interaction is deeper and more intimate. About Buddhism it could be said that Hinduism tried to reabsorb it with considerable success; having become a missionary religion it extended itself to foreign lands and flourished there more than in its homeland though its philosophy and general spirit helped in the revival and reformation of Hindu religion and society.

I have drawn attention to these historical facts in order to illustrate my theme that the specific genius of India is toleration and accommodation through evolutionary and peaceful change, and not swallowing up, digesting, assimilating, annihilating diversities and differences. That does not mean that assimilation has not taken place to a certain degree; in a long drawn-out historical process a common ground for all the religions and communities of India was being created and enlarged constantly, gradually and almost invisibly through a sharing of values, attitudes and ways of living. It is the same accommodating and sharing process that has been at work in India with regard to the Muslims also.

To understand the position of Islam in India it is necessary to delve a little into history. As it was with Christianity, the religion of Islam came to India prior to the sword and the politics of Islam. During the first flush of Islamic expansionism, Mohammed-bin-Kasim conquered Sind in 712 A.D., almost at the same time that the armies of Islam had entered Spain and reached the borders of France. But the attempt to conquer India stopped in Sind, and it was only after a few centuries that the next wave of Islamic invasion rolled into northern India. Before that in the 7th century, Islam had arrived in the Malabar coast in the southwest of India in a peaceful way through the Arab and Persian traders. It was not really a new phenomenon, but the continuation of the historic intercourse, now with a new Islamic content, that Arabs had maintained with the Malabar coast for a long period. The Hindu rulers of the Malabar coast welcomed the Arab traders, and the new religion they brought with them. Large numbers of them settled down in Kerala, married local women and converted many Hindus to Islam. The story is told of the last King of the Chera dynasty who became a Muslim and went to Arabia, and sent to Malabar missionaries who converted many Hindu families to Islam. The Muslims of what is now the state of Kerala known as Mapilas, had considerable influence in the court of the Hindu king, the Zamorin of Calicut.

By the 10th and 11th centuries Arab Muslims arrived in the east coast of India also. It was probably for them a half-way house in the shipping trade to China. In due course many conversions took place and by the 12th century there was a considerable Muslim community in the east coast. It is said that when the Pandya king died in 1293 A.D., he was succeeded by a Muslim who was an advisor in the court, the king's brother becoming his Minister.

I have narrated this early story of Islam in order to show that far from opposing the new religion of Islam it was welcomed and even encouraged by the rulers and the upper classes in South India. The simplicity and the fervour that marked the new religion, combined with the culture of the Arabs already not unfamiliar in the south and the advantage of trade they brought, all appealed to the people of southern India.

It is well known that Islamic ideas had their impact on Hindu thought in the south. The Bhakti cult which emerged later was a product of that influence. But it is not so well known that Sankara who rehabilitated Hinduism and made it triumph over Buddhist protestantism, was influenced by Islam. Some writers have ascribed to Islamic influence Sankara's opposition to the pluralist thought in Hinduism, his monism and his repudiation of the duality of godhead. Of course he could have derived these from the Upanishads, but it is possible that the impact of the new and vigorous ideas brought by Islam had helped in the sharpening of his monistic philosophy. That Sankara was excommunicated by the Brahmins gives some credence to this interpretation. There is an apocryphal story that the king of Kaladi, where Sankara was born, was converted to Islam. There is no doubt that Islamic religion and thought had created some sort of a stir in the south.

Islam, in turn, was powerfully influenced by Hindu culture, customs and manners enabling the two communities to live together in peace and harmony. It was only in the 14th century that the sword of Islam came to the south through the military campaigns of Malik Kafur and only in the 20th century that the politics of the Muslim League intruded into the region. But even then the fundamental tolerance and co-existence of the two religious communities has remained the broad fact of life in the south.

Far from being at logger-heads Indian and the Arab-Islamic worlds have had prolonged experience of each other in friendly intercourse, in the exchange of a wide variety of goods and the wealth of ideas. Steel, swords, gold and precious stones were brought from India by Arab merchants. Hindu and Buddhist treatises on astronomy, mathematics, medicine, logic and military sciences were translated into Arabic. The zero, the minus sign, the decimal place system and algebraic symbols passed from India to Arabia and thence to Europe. In architecture the pointed arch and the bulbous dome had their origins in India. The great story book "Panchtantra" was translated by the Arabs. It is told that the use of rosary was introduced to the Arab lands by Buddhist monks. Many were the positive results of the meeting between India and Islam.

From the 10th century onwards a new period of

turbulence set in this relationship in northern India. The Muslim conquerors who came from the northwest were not Arabs but belonged to the Turco-Afghan-Mongol tribes. New converts to Islam, they came not as traders and missionaries but as military and political conquerors at a time when India, after the dissolution of the empire of Harsha, presented a picture of internecine disorder and conflict in politics, and of rigidity and degeneration in religion and society. In eastern India the contest between Hinduism and Buddhism was still in progress and it is said that the Buddhist masses welcomed the Islamic conquerors with large numbers of them embracing Islam. These new conquerors were not purveyors of culture like the Arab Muslims who had come earlier to India, except, of course, for the sophisticated Persian influence from the northwest. They were possessed of the zeal of the newly converted. The confrontation in this period between Hinduism and Islam was therefore harsh, not only militarily and politically, but culturally and philosophically, Islam having by this time moved away from its original simplicity and evolved a rigorous religious-ethical-legal code. In this context Hinduism began to withdraw into a shell of self-protectionism resulting in social and cultural degeneration.

After absorbing the first shock waves of the Islamic conquest Hinduism began to assert itself, and in due course Hindus and Muslims began to search for a modus vivendi, which led to the evolution of a composite Hindu-Muslim culture in northern India. In the religious field it led to a limited and fragile synthesis, but in the field of culture it saw a cross-fertilization producing an efflorescence that was original and magnificent. The great temples, mosques, palaces, tombs and cenotaphs of the period were no longer purely Hindu or Islamic in style but a brilliant blending of the two. Painting and music were influenced by Islamic as well as Hindu traditions. It was not only in the higher arts but in the daily lives of the people that the impact of Islam was felt, in customs, and manners, and in dress—the dress of the Mughal court became the livery of the royalty and nobility all over India. The Indian cuisine got some of the richest and most delicious dishes from the Islamic heritage. A vital contribution was in the field of languages. Sanskrit, Turkish and Persian began to yield place to regional languages, with Urdu emerging as the language of a composite Hindu-Muslim culture in northern India. It is important to recall that Muslims had also made significant contributions to the study of Sanskrit. At the instance of Akbar and Dara Shikoh, the Vedas, Upanishads and the Puranas were translated into Persian and some of the Islamic scholars did even write original works in Sanskrit. The interaction between Sanskrit and Persian contributed not only to the evolution of Hindi, now the national language of India, but to regional languages like Marathi and Bengali.

In the realm of religious thought and devotion Islam and Hinduism influenced each other in many profound as well as subtle ways involving the minds and hearts of the Indian masses. The Bhakti movement which spread to almost all parts of India was leavened by Sufism, while Sufism which derived its original inspiration from the Koran, was influenced by several streams of ideas running not only from neo-Platonism and Christianity but from Hinduism and Buddhism. It may be said that the twin cults of Bhakti and Sufism, Hinduism and Islam had tried to reach out to each other for a religious as well as emotional rapprochement and synthesis. The names of Ramananda and Kabir are glorious examples of this.

"Kabir's" wrote Dr. Tarachand, "was the first attempt to reconcile Hinduism and Islam; the teachers of the south had absorbed Muslim elements, but Kabir was the first to come forward boldly to proclaim a religion of the center, a middle path, and his cry was taken up all over India and was re-echoed from a hundred places. He has numerous Hindu and Muslim disciples. . . . and his influence continued to spread under the Moghal rule, till a wise sovereign correctly estimating its value attempted to make it a religion approved by the State. Akbar's Dini-i-Ilahi was not an isolated freak of an autocrat. . . . but an inevitable result of forces which were deeply surging in India's breast, and finding expression in teachings of men like Kabir."*

Though the Sufies became the missionaries of Islam in India, making Islam appealing to the Indian masses, by the time Akbar boldly gave a new form to it in the eclectic religion of Din-i-Ilahi, Islamic orthodoxy began to look upon it with suspicion as something subversive of the true religion. The eclecticism of Akbar and the emotional harmonization attempted by Kabir began to be gradually rejected by Islamic orthodoxy once the grip of these great men flagged on the levers of power and the minds of the masses. But these ideas have not died altogether; they may hold relevance for the future, not for the same sort of religious unification or cultural assimilation, but for providing a philosophical basis and an emotional climate for realising in practice the age-old dream of unity in diversity. It was this dream that the wisest of the Muslim and the Hindu rulers and the greatest saints, thinkers and poets of India pursued in the more glorious periods of our history. The great Muslim emperors and thinkers did this because,

The influence of Islam on Indian Culture. Tarachand. The Indian Press (Publications Ltd.) Allahabad 1954. Page 165.

unlike the British whose main interests lay in their own country, they owed their allegiance to India and had no reason to suppress or exploit India for the benefit of any foreign power. They were thus interested in tackling the central problems of Indian life especially the question of reconciling the interests of social groups, regions and religions and providing the basis of a functioning unity for the empire or the nation.

When the British gained dominance over India, the Muslims, especially the aristocratic and the upper classes who had lost their ruling power, began retreating, almost like the Hindus during the early period of Islamic dominance, into a defensive shell shunning even western education and knowledge. On their part the British tried to weaken the economic position of Muslims and to exclude them from positions of political and administrative power. After the great rebellion of 1857, the British dealt with the Muslims with a heavier hand. Up to the end of the 19th century, Britain looked upon Indian Muslims as a potential source of danger to the empire. This policy began to change once a Hindu middle-class moved by sentiments of nationalism emerged. Official patronage then shifted back to the Muslims. The creation of the Muslim League in 1906 was a watershed in Indian history. In effect, first by patronising the Hindus, then the Muslims and actively helping to widen the rift between Hindus and Muslims, British rule arrested the historical process of mutual accommodation between the two communities which was at work during several centuries, and introduced in its place the imperial policy of divide and rule.

By this time a new consciousness had arisen among the Muslims of India. Sir Syed Ahmed Khan, the founder of the Aligarh Muslim University, urged the Muslims to abandon their attitude of aloofness from the British and to imbibe western education and scientific knowledge, while holding on to Islamic religion, law, customs and manners. He advised them to keep away from the Indian National Congress. He believed that representative government, which the Congress was demanding, would in due course lead to Hindu domination and that India, with all its multifarious differences in religion, language etc., was not suited to be governed by the western form of democratic government—a theme Mohammed Ali Jinnah later took up in his demand for Pakistan. Sir Mohamed Iqbal, the great poet of Islam, had also doubts about the applicability of democracy in India arguing that "the principle of European democracy cannot be applied to India without recognising the fact of communal groups." Iqbal had endorsed the demand for Pakistan.

It is interesting that after Pakistan was carved out of the body-politic of India as a sovereign state homogenous in the religious composition of its population, democracy and representative institutions could not function in Pakistan for long, while they did and do function in India inspite of the facts of communal and other groups and a variety of linguistic and regional differences. Indeed India has today a slightly larger Islamic population than Pakistan. Again, the fact of Islamic homogeneity did not prevent the eastern part of Pakistan from breaking away and forming the state of Bangladesh on nationalistic, political and economic grounds.

One may point out here that it is democracy with its central provision of the right to vote in free elections that turned out to be the best guarantee for the interests of minorities in India, especially of the Muslims. The notion that the majority community viz. the Hindus would cast their votes all in the same way and for the same party, and that the Indian National Congress as well as other political parties would not have to depend on the Muslim vote was a basic misconception. It is true that democratic politics today has thrown up regional, religious and caste forces in Indian politics. But notwithstanding such recrudescence of sectional interests, the system of universal adult suffrage and the freedom to exercise the vote have served to protect and promote the interests of the minorities, especially of an immense minority like the Muslims which is a major electoral force to be reckoned with.

I have argued that throughout history India has responded to the challenge of its multi-religious, multi-ethnic predicament not by the all-absorbing process of assimilation but by the strategy of toleration and by building up a society that is luxuriantly pluralistic. It is the same concept, in a modern form, that is embodied in the Indian Constitution. The Constitution provides for the preservation and promotion of the religious and cultural rights of the minorities, gives freedom to religious groups to pursue and propagate their religions, to manage their own religious affairs and to establish and maintain institutions of their own. This autonomy in the realm of religion and culture for minorities and groups is provided in the context of all-encompassing guarantees for everyone for equal protection before the law and against discrimination on grounds of religion, race, caste, sex or place of residence. In addition, there are the basic political rights to vote and freedom of speech and association and other rights associated with democracy. It is through this combination of minority rights with the general rights of the citizen that the Indian Constitution has sought to maintain a pluralist society protecting the religion and culture of groups while promoting the rights and interests of all.

Between the constitutional provisions and actual practices, there often falls the shadow, and no one claims that we
in India have fully succeeded in achieving in practice the
economic and social objectives we have set out for ourselves. I would, however, claim that we have made some
notable progress and it is in the direction of these objectives
that we have been moving by virtue of deliberate policies
and actions, and by the historic impulses in our society. The
ideal of a secular society that we have chosen for ourselves
has been supported by a ceaseless campaign against
communalism. It was clear to us that as a result of
independence and partition, Islamic communalism in India
had exhausted its momentum and it was by curbing the
communalism of the majority religion that a resurgence of
the former could be pre-vented and our secular democracy
safeguarded and strengthened.

There has been in India a revival of religious and
cultural consciousness in all communities as a by-product of
the growth of nationalism and sub-nationalism, and as a
result of economic and social development itself. This seems
to be happening almost everywhere in the world. There has
been the growth of fundamentalism in almost all parts of the
world, be it Islamic Middle East, or Christian America.
Even in communist countries such as the Soviet Union,
Eastern European countries and China, revivalism of one
kind or another is taking place. There is a Hindu revival and
an Islamic revival in India, but it is more in the social and
cultural fields than in the form of religious fanatacism
linked to politics or as fundamentalism of the type that is
manifesting itself in some of the Muslim countries. It is true
that communal incidents involving violence have occurred
in parts of India from time to time but their origins have

been more often political and economic than religious, and they have never been too frequent or widespread and have been always condemned and opposed by the government and the major political parties. Considering the size and complexity of India, what is remarkable is the religious and communal peace that has prevailed in the country since the stormy aftermath of partition.

There are, of course, many problems and disabilities that the Islamic population of India experiences, but most of them they share with the majority of the people of the country. Basically they are part of the general and gigantic problems of poverty, disease and ignorance, in short, of development and adjustment of an old society to modernization—problems faced by all the people of India. However, the impact of the general problems on different communities and sections of society vary in intensity according to the objective situation of the community in question. Greater representation in government services and legislatures is a major demand—it is a question that affects all in a developing society with a huge population and with not enough jobs like India, but the demand of the Muslims has been recognized as deserving urgent attention. The Muslims, in comparison to upper class Hindus, were left behind in education when almost in proud disdain they kept themselves aloof from the modern education introduced by the British. Some of the social customs like purdah for women had affected their progress and adjustment to modern times. Islamic personal law is another question. In spite of the constitutional provision that "The State shall endeavour to secure for the citizens a uniform social code throughout the territory of India," the state in India has not tried to do this in deference to a consensus among its Muslim population that the State should not pass legislation for reforming the traditional Islamic personal law. That would indeed be considered as interfering in the realm of laws and practices allowed by religion. The State, therefore, is obliged to leave alone this legislative task until opinion among the Indian Muslims evolves and initiates a demand for such reforms. There is today growing opinion among Muslim youth that unless there is some reform in this field, Indian Muslims will not be able to cope with the changes being brought about by modernization.

This is a problem affecting Islam not only in India but in some Islamic countries as well. In India the majority community also, in spite of legal reforms, are in fact constricted by many traditional customs and practices that impede their adjustment to the requirements of modernization. For Indian Muslims language is a sensitive issue, especially in northern India as language is a cultural and emotional issue for every major linguistic group in India. It may be mentioned that the language spoken by Muslims in various Indian States is the regional language and not Urdu except in parts of northern India, though they tend to learn Urdu also. By and large, India has dealt with the problem of langauge with tolerance and understanding. Urdu occupies a major position in India today and is recognized in the Constitution as one of the regional languages. In fact, in Northern India, Urdu is the repository of the composite Hindu-Muslim culture and is a potential instrument for promoting unity rather than division. Promotion of Urdu is an aspiration of the Indian Muslims which has been recognized and which it is in the interest of the composite culture of India to be developed to its fullest potentialities.

Transcending language and customs and manners, indeed religion itself, is the general and often somewhat vague aspiration of the Muslims of India to preserve their identity as Muslims. This struggle for the preservation of identity is, first of all, in relation to the sea of Hindu humanity surrounding them, and secondly, in relation to the tide of modernization that is sweeping across the country. As I said earlier, all sectors of Indian society are facing the same problem in varying degrees of intensity. Even Hindus, certainly the more orthodox ones, are struggling to maintain some of their age-old customs and beliefs against the onslaught of modernism. There are several factors that put the efforts of the Islamic community in India in a favourable context. In the first place, 80 million people are no ordinary minority that can be ignored and their desires and demands will have to be responded to. Secondly, democracy and secularism and the tradition of toleration of a multi-religious society have provided the legal framework as well as the mental climate for maintaining the identity of the Muslims as well as that of other religious groups in India. Thirdly, the peaceful method and the almost Fabian gradualness of India's technological modernization, though considerable in its totality and impressive in its results, provide a certain cushioning not only for the Muslims but the majority community of the Hindus to adjust to change more painlessly than was possible in the recklessly unplanned and undemocratic industrialization of the early capitalist period, and the forced and violent experiments in economic transformation carried out elsewhere. And finally, the Indian Muslims, even after partition, have cast their lot with India and have become an immense and indispensable constituent of the complex Indian system.

A perceptive Australian scholar, who is present today at this conference, conducted a study some years ago of Muslim communities in two cities in India—one in Madhya

Pradesh and the other in Tamil Nadu. "At every point," he wrote, "that has a substantial bearing on their position as citizens of a secular republic, ordinary Muslims emerge in the study reported here, not as one would have been led to expect, as members of a monolithic community sitting sullenly apart, but as active participants in regional cultures whose perspectives they share."* This is true of the attitude and the role of Muslims not only in regional cultures but in Indian culture as a whole. Today, thanks to all-India elections and all-India planning for economic and social development, and to a foreign policy which opened the windows of the nation to the winds of development from the world over, India as an entity and as an experience impinges on every Indian wherever he may live and whichever religion or community he may belong to. Developmental programmes in the Five Year Plans have been responsible more than anything else in putting an economic content in Indian unity which neither Asoka nor Akbar nor the British Raj could attempt or achieve. It is in this context of traditionally inherited toleration, of more recently established democracy, and the new facts of economic unity and inter-dependence that the Muslims of India have come to share a common destiny with other Indians and become an indispensable and integral part of our nation of 700 million people.

---

*Peter B. Mayer "Tombs and Dark Houses: Ideology, Intellectuals and Politicians in the Study of Contemporary Indian Islam." Journal of Asian Studies—May 1981, Vol: XI, No. 3.

VIII
Remembering Ambedkar

I am happy that various Indian associations in New York irrespective of religion, sect, caste or creed and including a good number of Americans have associated themselves with this meeting to mark the 92nd birthday of Dr. B. R. Ambedkar.

Dr. Ambedkar was one of the giants of our time, one of the great personalities of the Indian national movement and of the Indian renaissance. He was a many-splendoured personality, a great scholar, an original thinker, writer, orator, debater, a great jurist and constitutionalist, and above all a restless agitator and revolutionary working for social reform and radical social changes in our country.

I recall the brief meeting I had with Ambedkar in New Delhi in 1943 when he was a member of the Viceroy's Executive Council. After taking my first degree from Travancore I had gone to the north in search of a job. I had a letter of introduction to Ambedkar from one who had known him in Travancore. I took a room in a cheap hotel in Delhi, put my luggage there and then went to Ambedkar's

Speech at meeting on April 12, 1983, organized in New York by Indian associations on the 92nd birth anniversary of Dr. B. R. Ambedkar.

residence at Prithvi Raj road with the introduction letter. He read the letter and asked me "where are your 'sammans,' your luggage?" Obviously he was thinking of putting me up at his residence. That was the kind of human being that he was. Though I was a stranger coming from a remote corner of Kerala he wanted to put me up in his house.

India was fortunate to have a crop of great leaders during this century. I would put Ambedkar on the same level with them, with Gandhi, Nehru, Jinnah and others. As you know there were many differences and great debates among those leaders, but all of them were united on two things—freedom for India, and except for Jinnah, the unity of India.

Ambedkar hated the caste system, "untouchability" and the inequalities of old Indian society with a glowing, incandescent hatred. He fought those social ills and injustices ruthlessly and with unmatched political skill. But that did not prevent him from remaining a staunch Indian nationalist. What he was trying was to bargain, and he was a tough bargainer, with the British and other Indian nationalist leaders for the maximum that he could get for his community in terms of political safeguards. That was his intention and not to compromise on Indian independence. As a shrewd politician he used the opportunity offered by the period of transition from foreign rule to independence for getting maximum benefits and safeguards for his community *viz.* the Scheduled Castes or Harijans as Mahatma Gandhi called them. We all know how Gandhiji was dedicated to the abolition of "untouchability," how he tried to arouse among Hindus a sense of shame in regard to this social evil and urged them into social action to remove it.

The Scheduled Castes are still the lowest, the most

deprived, the most dispossessed and the least educated section of Indian society. They were shaken up as were the rest of the Indian masses by the nationalist movement. If Mahatma Gandhi introduced a moral purpose, shall one say a moral soul, as well as a mass dimension to the Indian nationalist movement, and if Jawaharlal Nehru introduced a social and economic dimension and a world vision, Dr. Ambedkar brought to it a profound social content and a passionate protest against social inequalities and oppression. If Gandhiji aroused the masses of India as a whole, Ambedkar aroused and organized social and political consciousness among the lowest strata of Indian society. Our democracy is functioning properly in India because the masses, the average voter, is able to cast his vote with a degree of intelligence and political consciousness. Today the voter from this lowest strata of society is able to exercise his right to vote properly partly due to the work done by Dr. Ambedkar in arousing their consciousness.

There were some people who questioned the nationalism of Dr. Ambedkar. I happened to have read Ambedkar somewhat carefully. As early as in the 1930s Ambedkar had said, and I quote: "To say that this country is divided by castes and creeds and that it cannot be one united self-governing community unless adequate safeguards for protection of minorities are made as part of the constitution, is a position to which there can be no objection; but the minorities must bear in mind that although today we are riven by and atomised by caste, our ideal is a united India. That being so, it follows that every minority in formulating the safeguards it needs must take care that they will not be incompatible with the realization of this great ideal."

That was a statement Ambedkar made in the

impassioned days of bitter political debates with Gandhiji. There could be no doubt that he stood for a free India, for a united India. Again in 1949 delivering his great speech during the third reading of free India's Constitution, he put forward the same position on freedom and unity. There was an admirable consistency about the man. He warned the Constituent Assembly: "What perturbs me greatly is the fact that India has not only once before lost her independence but she lost it by the infidelity and treachery of its own people." He then exhorted every party not to place its particular beliefs above the interests of the nation, and said: "We must be determined to defend our independence till the last drop of our blood." Could there be any more passionate declaration of nationalism and patriotism than this?

Dr. Ambedkar was, of course, a great democrat. His contribution to Indian democracy was not limited to his high position as the Chairman of the Drafting Committee of the Constitution and to his skillful role in piloting the draft of the Constitution in the Constituent Assembly. He had during his political career put forward a variety of political and social ideas that fertilized Indian thinking and contributed to our decision to adopt the parliamentary form of democracy for India. In the speech I quoted earlier, which was the last one he made on the Constitution before it was passed, he gave a warning: "On January 26, 1950 we will have equality in politics and inequality in social and economic life. We must remove this contradiction at the earliest moment or else those who suffer from inequality will blow up the structure of political democracy which this Assembly has so laboriously built up." In that speech he used a colourful phrase. He said that political democracy erected on the divisions, inequalities and injustices of traditional Indian society would be like "a palace built on cow-dung." Cow-dung may be sacred and useful, but very fragile. I should like to add here that democracy has survived in India because the leadership of new India managed to introduce a meaningful social and economic content into our system of political democracy.

A lot is written in books on what the British did during the Raj to improve the lot of "the untouchables." They did something no doubt, they were a long time in India. But the basic attitude of the British rulers of India was one of neutrality on fundamental religious and social questions. They adopted this neutrality because they did not wish to offend and antagonize powerful sections of Indian society constituting the wealthier classes and the upper castes; their main interest was to maintain their rule undisturbed by social or political opposition. Dr. Ambedkar had something telling to say about this policy of social neutrality. He remarked that the British attitude was like that of a Chinese tailor (not a tailor from today's People's Republic of China), who when given cloth to make a suit together with an old suit as a model, made the new suit so faithfully according to the old model with all its stains, tears and patches! That was, Ambedkar said, what the British did to the old Indian social system; they preserved almost everything they inherited. Of course some minor social reforms were introduced and forces of change were also at work in Indian society following the introduction of modern industry. There was, however, no policy of social change or any attempt to tamper with the social system.

One of his biographers has narrated the story of Ambedkar's audience with King George V during the Round Table Conference in London. Sitting in the garden of Buckingham Palace the King-Emperor asked Dr.

Ambedkar about the condition of "the untouchables" in
India and Ambedkar gave a telling picture of their squalid
life in Indian society. The biographer says that George V
shuddered at this narration. Now, one knows that the King
was genuinely moved, but was it the British Government
and not the Indian people or Mahatma Gandhi who was
ruling India then? That was really the attitude of the British
Raj on basic social questions. The British were around in
India since Clive won the battle of Plassey in 1757, and
Queen Victoria became the Empress of India in 1876.
Though they ruled India for well over a century, they could
still disown responsibility for all of India's social ills. I am
not denying the Indian responsibility for them during the
colonial period or even after, but am merely pointing out
how significant social reforms and changes could not take
place in India during the period of the British Raj.

In his great speech in the Constituent Assembly,
Ambedkar warned the newly emerged independent nation
of three dangers. One was the danger to constitutional
government. He pleaded that we must always stick to
constitutional methods for achieving our objectives—
political, social or economic. It is interesting that this social
revolutionary who passionately criticized the Hindu social
system, prescribed constitutional methods alone for cor-
recting those ills and effecting social and economic development. He was opposed to the method of Satyagraha that
Gandhi preached and practised; he said that Satyagraha—
nonviolent non-cooperation—meant anarchy and that it
should not be practised in independent India. Ambedkar
was a democrat and a constitutionalist in the classical sense
of the term.

The second danger he warned India against was hero
worship. He pointed out that India was prone to the Bhakti

cult—the cult of religious devotion—and tended to worship our leaders as heroes. That, according to Ambedkar was not in conformity with the principles of democracy. He quoted the famous words of the Irish patriot Daniel O'Connor that "A man should not be grateful at the cost of his honour, a woman at the cost of her chastity and a nation at the cost of its liberty." He exhorted India never to put its liberty at the feet of any man however great and surrender its freedom and liberty.

Ambedkar's third exhortation was on the need for state action for removing the inherited ills and evils of Indian society especially untouchability and the caste system. Gandhiji had opposed and fought against untouchability more than anyone else in Indian history. He was a crusader against untouchability. As regards the caste system, though he was opposed to its degeneration and rigorous distinctions, Gandhi was not fundmentally opposed to the system as such. It was Ambedkar who advocated a root and branch change in the caste system, its abolition in theory and practice, indeed its destruction. Age-old prejudices and social practices die hard in practice. Today if you read the matrimonial columns of ethnic Indian newspapers published in America, you will find the influence of caste even among Indians living abroad.

Some speakers before me have talked about the problem of caste in India today. It is not easy in practice to remove completely within a short period age-old social customs. You know how in the Civil War in America the question of slavery and the liberation of the Negroes was one of the great issues. This great democracy with all its affluence and stability has yet to root out completely social, economic and psychological distinctions arising from this old inequality.

One will have some idea of the enormity of the tasks faced by India during the last 34 years of freedom if one views it with a bit of sympathetic imagination, how we have been, for the frist time in hundreds of years of foreign invasions and foreign rule, trying to reform a society which had almost got frozen in social backwardness. We have to change an ancient society which did not have the chance of normal evolution in history and to eradicate from the minds and hearts of people deeply rooted social prejudices and attitudes. Thanks to Gandhi, Nehru, Ambedkar and other leaders, untouchability has been abolished in law by the Constitution and made a justiceable offence, and there is provision for reservations in government services and educational institutions for the Scheduled Castes and Tribes. The Directive Principles of the Constitution also provide for special measures for the upliftment socially, educationally and economically of the weaker sections of society. For the first time there is a legislative state in India established by the Constitution in the drafting of which Ambedkar had a major role.

In the British period there was no such legistlative state in India though some pieces of social legislation were introduced by them, like the prohibition of Sati and child marriage. But then let us not forget it was at the instance of Indian reformers like Raja Ram Mohan Roy and others, indeed on the urgings of the enlightened sections of the Indian public, that such legislation was brought about by the British. Today, the State in India has become an instrument of social and economic change. We still suffer from many social inequalities and problems and new conflicts among sections of people, among castes and other interest groups, have arisen, based more on economic factors. India today is at a new stage of development and some of these conflicts are partly due to the process of development itself, due to the rise in the consciousness and expectations of people.

The progress that the ordinary masses and the deprived sections of society have made in India since Independence is not negligible, it is remarkable compared to the relatively short span of time and the huge magnitude of the problems involved. Even richer societies which had similar problems of social distinctions have not yet fully overcome them. The Scheduled Castes in India whose cause Ambedkar espoused, are still the victims in practice of social and economic deprivations but they have made considerable progress since Independence, and above all they are today conscious of their rights. India has Cabinet Ministers, High Court Judges, even a Supreme Court Justice, Ambassadors and many high officials belonging to this section of our population. Dr. Ambedkar said that he was surprised when he was asked soon after Independence to become a member of the Drafting Committee on the Constitution, that he was even more surprised when he was asked to be the Chairman of the Committee and then the Law Minister of India. Mr. Jagjivan Ram, another member of the Scheduled Castes, was a member of the Cabinet right from the beginning and he later became a Deputy Prime Minister of India.

All this does not mean that the Scheduled Castes have got over their social and economic problems. We in India recognize these problems which are immense, but one must also recognize the progress that has been made. Ambedkar's work was one of the most powerful forces behind the social change that has come over India not only for the Scheduled Castes and Tribes but for the deprived sections of the society as a whole.

I said earlier that Ambedkar was a great democrat. He

was very much attracted by the philosophy of equality in Buddhism and finally he became a Buddhist. Ambedkar once remarked that he studied many philosophies and creeds including Marxism and Communism. But he said he preferred to follow the path of the Buddha because it is "the safest and soundest" method.

IX
Multi-Lingual India

India can perhaps be described as a dome of many-coloured glass, iridescent and fragile in appearance, but elastic and unbreakable in substance. Multi-lingualism is merely a part of this bewildering and fascinating diversity of India. We have not only a multitude of tongues, but many faiths and religions and a variety of historical, social, cultural and racial elements that co-exist and interact with one another within a complex and comprehensive framework of unity.

At this learned and high-level Round Table, it is not necessary for me to narrate the basic facts about the languages of India: to say that we have over 1600 languages is to conjure up a frightening image of a country that is a veritable tower of Babel. However, as a matter of fact, over centuries, even without the modern means of communications, India had managed to exist as a cultural and civilizational entity, transmitting ideas, sentiments, myths, conventions and symbolism from one end to the other of this vast land, and also to countries in the neighbourhood

Speech on May 21, 1982, at the fourth South Asian Language Roundtable, Syracuse University, Syracuse, New York.

101

and farther away. Thus, though linguistic and other differences are baffling, what is remarkable is the essential thread of unity that runs through the foundations as well as the super-structure of our variegated culture and society. The 1600 odd languages belonging basically to three or four families of languages, articulate largely common or connected experiences, emotions and aspirations of the people, and constitute some kind of an oversized orchestra playing essentially the same tune, though from time to time a flute or a trumpet strikes a discordant note. Be it in Sanskrit, Hindi, Urdu, Punjabi, Marathi, Telugu or Tamil, it is the same or similar myths and stories, joys and sorrows, hopes and aspirations that are being expressed and communicated. It is important to emphasize this if one is to understand why the Indian system has survived substantially over the ages and is ticking today.

If there are 1652 languages in India, all except 15 are really minor languages or dialects. Fifteen languages are no doubt plenty enough for a country, but in comparison to the number of languages spoken in Europe and the size of the population of Europe, fifteen is not too intolerable a number for a population of 700 million. What is unique about India is that all these tongues are spoken under the umbrella of one sovereign State. A common language is not the hallmark of nationality. One can have different nations speaking the same language as in the Arab, Spanish and English-speaking worlds, and one can have a nation speaking different languages as is the case with Switzerland, Yugoslavia, the Soviet Union, and to some extent China. But it is true that the latter is a rarer and more difficult thing to achieve, and it is particularly difficult if one has 16 major languages to deal with, including English, as in India. To make matters even more complex, these languages belong to entirely different families like the Indo-Aryan, Dravidian and Mongoloid, and today each language represents a regional cultural revival and, sometimes, an assertive and fissiparous sub-nationalism tied to local economic and political interests. It would be naive to ignore the problems posed by this multi-lingual predicament of India. At the same time one must delve deeper into the situation to discover the common thread running through it all.

The linguistic picture of India is not as chaotic as it appears if it is realized that over 70% of the people speak an Indo-Aryan language, 20% Dravidian languages, and 2-3% English, a three percent that is widely, though thinly, spread out among the upper and middle classes across the board in the country. It is also important to realize that Sanskrit is at the base of the majority of India's national languages and has got itself interspersed with or superimposed on the remaining languages belonging to entirely different families. Further, one language, Hindi, which has been adopted as the official and the link language, is spoken by about 50% of the population amounting to over 350 million people, and is spreading and evolving almost before our very eyes notwithstanding regional obstacles and psychological resistance. It may be that these broad common factors somewhat simplify the complexity and confusion involved in the multi-lingual situation. It may be added that the scripts of the Indian languages bear basically the impress of the Bramhi script and this is said to be true not only of the scripts of the Indo-Aryan languages of the North but of the Dravidian languages of the South, and even of the Singhalese, Mon-Burmese, Cambodian-Siamese, and the Java-Balinese languages of South-East Asia. One would, however, freely grant that none of these broad and basic common characteristics of origin and influence make it, in a practical sense, easier for people to understand and speak the languages of one another. But inherent in these are the possibilities of promoting one link language for the whole of India.

I should like to stress here one curious historical fact. It has not been an uncommon experience in the history of India for the ruling elite and the upper classes to adopt a language of foreign origin as the link language. That was so with Sanskrit which was brought to India by the Aryans though its real and glorious development took place within India. Max Mueller had noted in the 19th century that more people in India understood Sanskrit then than people in Europe understood Latin during the time of Dante. Much earlier in the 9th century A.D. India witnessed the re-markable feat of Sankaracharya travelling from the southern tip of India to its northern end debating in Sanskrit with scholars with such persuasiveness as to bring about the revival of Hinduism not only among the elite but the masses. Sanskrit became the language of philosophy, religion and literature and the lingua franca of the learned. It also gave rise to the great north Indian languages and vitalised the other languages of India. Sanskrit has served the Indian people for over 3000 years and continues to be a great unifying factor in India. It is also a continuing link with important sections of the scholastic community in the rest of the world. I am not suggesting that Sanskrit be pushed aggressively, but only that the advantage of this great classical language, which is understood by more people in India than Greek and Latin in modern Europe, must be appreciated and utilized. Further, in the Devana-gari script, there exists a possible common script for other Indian languages though one cannot be too optimistic about the practicability of adopting it in view of the tenacious attachment of people to their own particular scripts.

Another link language which flourished in India was Persian which in its interplay with Sanskrit and Arabic, produced the great modern language, Urdu. Here again beginning as a court or camp language, it blossomed into a modern tongue of the people, linking India linguistically with the Arab world.

The third link language of foreign origin is, of course, English. It is obvious that English acts as a unifying force in India, as the language of administration, as a lingua franca, and as a medium of modern knowledge and ideas in the realm of politics and society, and especially in the field of science and technology. English has also evolved as a language of literature in India, and like Sanskrit and Persian in the past, it has helped the evolution as well as the systematisation of several regional languages of India. Today one may say that English has become an Indian language spoken by 15-20 million people, which is about the size of the population of English-speaking Australia. It is recognized today as an additional official language, and its role as a link language within India and as an international language for India, is so compelling that policy-wise as well as pragmatically, it is bound to occupy an important place in India.

However, English cannot continue indefinitely as the premier official language or lingua franca of India. This is so because, as Jawaharlal Nehru said: "It is an obvious thing and a vital thing that any country, much more so a free and independent country, must function in its own language." Thus free Indians cannot be imitation Englishmen, but just as Sanskrit or Persian did not detract from the evolution of Indianness, English need not necessarily make Indians less

Indian. It is true that in the 19th century, English education did produce an educated elite who had some of the characteristics of counterfeit Englishmen. Even then Indian culture, religion and nationalism had made them a new specimen of composite human beings rather than synthetic Englishmen. One interesting feature of the current cultural scene in India is that the English-educated Indian is more and more a bilingual or a trilingual Indian, and his religious, social and cultural beliefs and habits are more indigenous than foreign. The power of the traditional genius of India to absorb speech and ideas from outside without sacrificing the basic values and patterns of Indian life and culture is shown in regard to English language and culture as well.

I have dealt in some detail with India's historical experience with languages of foreign origin in order to drive home the point that far from being alienating factors, they can be unifying and enlightening influences in our society. In a sense they have broadened the basis of Indian unity and also built up a thinly but widely spread superstructure of inter-communication. At the same time none of these link-languages, not even Hindi, can push aside the vibrant national or regional languages of India. Far from attempting any such thing, it has been our State policy to recognize them as national languages, to encourage their growth and development, to allow them to be used for education and administration in the States concerned, as well as in the Central Parliament, if one so desired. The constitutionally-recognized 15 national languages have been so well-developed during the last 800 or 1000 years, flourishing as major literatures during the last one century, and experiencing a new efflorescense since Independence, that they are today vital linguistic, cultural and political forces to be reckoned with. And besides they are spoken by populations larger than those of many independent countries in the world—around 45 million for Telugu, 45 million for Bengali, 42 million for Gujarati, 22 million for Malayalam and 22 million for Kannada etc. It is, therefore, practically inconceivable to give them anything but the fullest freedom of usage and development.

Ever since Independence India has been wrestling with the problems posed by this multilingual situation. It was realized that the solution did not lie in promoting even a national language like Hindi as an official or link language at the expense of any other national-regional language. At the same time, it was understood that English could not continue to play indefinitely the role of official language in independent India, and that Hindi, which is spoken by the largest percentage of people and with roots in India's ancient culture, can be the only credible alternative. However, as Nehru realized: "Any attempt to impose a particular language on an unwilling people has usually met with the strongest opposition and has actually resulted in something the reverse of what the promoters thought." By and large almost every region of India has accepted the pre-eminence of Hindi, but there are differences over the degree, the pace and the methods of promoting it. If there is the inevitability of gradualness in any field of development, it is in the learning of a langauge by a whole nation. If a completely alien tongue like English could be learned by a good cross-section of the upper and middle classes, there is no reason that Hindi, which is a national language spoken by over 200 million people, should not be learnt as an official and link language by Indians as a whole. Only, the methods of propagating it required understanding of the psychology of linguistic groups, and appreciation of the fact that the dissemination of a language is essentially an evolutionary process, though it can be speeded up by governmental policies as well as voluntary action by the people.

As pointed out earlier Hindi is already spoken by nearly 50 percent of the people of India. In spite of periodical resistance from some states, Hindi has in fact spread in the south of India much more rapidly than has been commonly understood. In another twenty years or so it is reasonable to expect that the South will speak as much Hindi as it speaks English today without probably abandoning English. Hindi, in spite of the restrictive search for a puristic model, has shown itself to be a vital and growing language, at once a language of the books and a language of the mohallah and the market place. It has become already a major language of popular journalism. According to the annual reports of the Registrar of Newspapers, Hindi journals contributed the largest group in India increasing from 4196 newspapers in 1978 to over 5000 in 1982. In terms of circulation 100 Hindi papers held the lead with 13,709,000 copies in 1980. The largest number of daily papers, altogether 3644 was also published in Hindi. English was a close second in terms of the extent of circulation and the number of newspapers.

While the growth of popular Hindi journalism is noteworthy, it is equally important that through film and radio a simple version of Hindi is getting down to the people all over India in a pleasant and acceptable way. For the dissemination of Hindi to the widest extent possible, Jawaharlal Nehru had once suggested that distinction be made between Hindi as a regional language and as an all-India language. He suggested: "Let Hindi be developed as a regional langauge and made as rich as possible; but let a simpler form of Hindi be specially developed for all-India purposes for people to know easily. Let it consist of five thousand words, let us say, or six thousand or ten thousand words which would be quite enough for normal communication." That was a wise and pragmatic approach, and as a matter of fact it is in this simple form that Hindi has been evolving as a lingua franca among the people in addition to the book knowledge that is being imbibed in schools and colleges.

Hindi has also become an international language. It is indeed the third largest world language coming after Chinese and English in the sense of the number of people who speak it. People of Indian descent in many countries speak it as their mother tongue, and as a foreign language it is taught in 90 universities in different countries including the United States, the Soviet Union and several European countries. Indeed some of the regional languages of India like Tamil, Telugu, Malayalam, Marathi and Punjabi have also become international languages in the same sense.

This spread of Hindi has not, however, solved the problem of an official language or a lingua franca for India in view of the powerful position occupied by the national languages in the States and regions, and the continuing unavoidability of English as a link language. We have wrestled with this issue for a long time and it has become clear that many languages like many religions have become an established fact of Indian life which is not necessarily a disturbing, fissiparous phenomenon. On the other hand it could be an enriching and enlivening factor of life. Of course it can be too enlivening when it erupts in the form of social and political tensions and agitations. However, considering the magnitude and the complexity of the problem what is remarkable about the Indian scene is multi-lingual co-existence rather than linguistic conflicts. Other countries with only two allied languages like English and French are not much better off than India in this respect.

The three-language formula that we have adopted is a pragmatic compromise approach, which may be burdensome for students but perhaps unavoidable in the linguistic predicament in which India finds itself. The difficulties of the situation are obvious, but nevertheless that is the only practical approach keeping in mind the pulls of linguistic nationalism, and the broader requirements of national unity and international communication. The use of the regional language, of Hindi as the official language, and of English as an additional official language, in education and administration at different stages or concurrently is a reflection of the facts as well as the requirements of Indian life. It is clear that the language question can be settled, or shall I say harmoniously adjusted, not merely as a result of State policy but as an evolutionary process. In the meantime, difficulties and tensions are bound to surface from time to time, but the ancient and essential cultural unity of India, and the present-day economic inter-dependence which has provided a new material basis for Indian unity, is strong enough to sustain the fabric of our society and nation. Above all, the democratic system has provided a method by which linguistic and other differences could be dealt with and reconciled peacefully, though "the wild freedoms of democracy," to use a Churchillian phrase, may make the process appear a little confused, but certainly very exciting.

X

Rationale of Nonalignment

I am very much honoured to have this opportunity to speak to the International Club. The Indian Embassy has had a long and fruitful relationship with this Club. We are actually a member of the family of the International Club and that is proved by the fact that several of my officers are present at this meeting. You have given me no subject to speak on, which is rather difficult. You have given me a long rope with the result I do not know where to go. Well, I should nevertheless like to say something.

India is a very old country with a very ancient history and we have gone through innumerable vicissitudes of life and history. We were open to the West, to the East, to the North and the South in our long history; India and India's policies cannot be understood except in the perspective of this history.

The other day I was reading a learned article on the origins of the domino theory in international politics. The author has traced it from the time of the Peloponnesian wars, from great men like Thucydides who advanced

Address to International Club of Washington, D.C. on November 10, 1983.

something like a domino theory without using the word at that time. It seems to be the lesson of history that we rarely learn from history. The thrust of this article was the tragic results of the domino theory as it was applied to the Greek States. Nations are often moved in their actions by some kind of domino theory or other in spite of the disastrous history of its consequences and its irrelevance to actual situations.

The history of Europe is full of lessons for us if only we are willing to pause and think a little. I read a fascinating book on the Thirty Years War, the great ideological war fought in Europe, the war between Catholics and Protestants in the 17th century. The historian C. V. Wedgwood, tracing the course of the war, points out how the nature of the war changed almost in midcourse, how the religious-ideological content got itself exhausted and how power politics and the play of nations against one another took the place of the ideological struggle with paradoxical results; how the Pope, the head of the Catholic Church, set himself against the Hapsburg Empire which stood for the crusade in favour of Catholicism, and how Catholic France under Cardinal Richelieu subsidized Protestant Sweden. And, instead of the terms Catholic and Protestant a new term emerged— Frenchmen, Swedes, Austrians, nationalism arose, and what was really begun as an ideological war ended up as a conflict of nations for a balance of power in Europe.

You can apply this almost exactly to what happened after the Second World War. You can look up what happened to the allies and what happened to the enemies they fought. Some of the allies have fallen out and have become mortal antagonists, not only ideologically but also in terms of military and political contest. Thus, until some years ago, just as in the Thirty Years War the Pope subsidized the Protestants, we found in the Communist bloc the Soviets and the Chinese falling out and in fact subsidizing others against each other. Today, of course, some of the old enemies are friends, whether it is Germany or Japan, and we hear how these countries are arming themselves or being urged to arm themselves again. And who can say for certain that today's friends and enemies will not change their roles five or ten years from now. I say this because someone had once said that Britain had no permanent friends or enemies but only permanent interests. I think today we are in an age when we have neither permanent enemies, nor permanent friends, and even no permanent interests as nations. This is the age in which the world, because of political, technological and social developments and the evoution of a global community, has developed common interests affecting humanity as a whole.

I mention this background because we in India were exposed in our history to various influences and differing and conflicting currents of history. Our own society was fashioned by all these and hence we have such bewildering varieties and differences. What we have striven is to live together, to co-exist in this vast, and often jarring diversity, even though our efforts were sometimes marred by tragic intervals of conflicts and bloodshed. If we have learnt anything, it is the inevitability of living together. This is true not only in the nuclear age, but, according to the lessons of history it was true even in the pre-nuclear age. Muslims and Christians fought a long crusade but they came to co-exist, as did Catholics and Protestants. They have come to co-exist not by succeeding to extinguish the other ideology or religion but by learning to tolerate each other.

Now India's own approach to the world is a product of our historical experience of almost being forced by history to co-exist and live together in the midst of such diversities and differences.

It was from this context that our policy of non-alignment and peaceful co-existence emerged. We were convinced, when faced with the new ideological contest of our times between communism and democracy or capitalistic democracy, that neither of the two would be able to destroy or extinguish the other, that sooner or later it was necessary, even inevitable, for the two camps to learn to live together. If that was necessary in the pre-nuclear age, it has become compulsory in the nuclear age. That was the broad international and philosophical context of India's policy of nonalignment and peaceful co-existence, which unfortunately was not understood by powers on both sides who were obsessed with antagonistic passions and the agony of accommodating with each other.

We did understand the intensity of the emotions and the ideas that divided the opposing camps; we were not trying as some people thought to take a superior moral position or sit on the fence, but were merely trying to project our own historical and domestic experience to the world problems of our time. Now, we know, and we have learnt by bitter experience that it is immensely difficult to operate a policy of this sort in a world where the contestants are not only just facing each other in opposition but are living in a world community that has become intricately interdependent. Of course the ideological conflict is still here. At the same time, the influences and ideas of each bloc have been penetrating the other and in a sense the pure and sharp ideological conflict has been overtaken by a power conflict.

India became independent in 1947 when China was still under Chiang kai-Shek, but the situation changed very drastically after China turned communist in 1949. Then it was thought by the West that maybe it was not a bad idea to have India as a nonaligned country and a democratic country. And to some extent I think we had, in a political sense, a certain weight or influence in the international balance, not in terms of power or economics, but in a psychological, political sense. After China became communist, India could have, to some degree at least, tilted the political balance of the world if it has joined one side or the other in the cold war. But we came to the conclusion that even in power-politcal terms a tilting of the balance in this way would have been injurious to the peace and stability of the world. We had other and even more important considerations in not choosing one side or other. We were at that time a pioneer in the emerging third world—the first big country which emerged from colonialism. We looked around and we saw that there were millions of people who were struggling for freedom from colonial empires of one great power or other, and we believed that if these new nations could avoid being sucked into the power politics and military alliances of one bloc or another, there might emerge an area of peace as a cushion between the two contending blocs. If one considers that the majority of mankind even today lives outside the system of great-power military alliances, one would see that there was some sense in this idea of creating a political-psychological cushion between the two ideological-military blocs. We believe that to a modest extent we contributed to the relief of tensions and to the prevention of polarization of the world into two sharply warring camps. If the world succeeded in preserving peace, at least world peace if not regional peace, for the last forty years, the refusal of the majority of the new emerging nations to join with one bloc or another was one of the factors that contributed to it. Of course there were other factors, maybe more important power factors—I would really concede this—but the nonalignment of the new nations also had a pacifying role.

We are today living in a world, where though power is concentrated, in a nuclear sense, in two centers, in a political sense there is a diffusion of power in the world. There are small countries and middle countries which can obstruct the great nations, which can prevent or at least delay something or the other from happening that would make use of them as instruments or arenas of conflict. Very often India's policy in this regard has been criticized as either sitting on the fence, or sheer hypocrisy or as not being even-handed between the two power centers.

In my opinion we have to be judged mainly by what we are doing internally in India. This is the real test of what India is. We are a democracy but we are not interested in a crusade of democracy, in imposing our democracy on others or in joining in any crusade for that. But we are passionately interested in strengthening the foundations of democracy in our country, in making it an enduring, working system, and in defending it. For this we had to adopt many methods, many stratagems, because we were a poor country faced with innumerable problems when we became independent and if there is any miracle today in India, it is that in a developing country with so many inherited problems of poverty and inequality and all manner of differences we have been able to establish a democratic system on the basis of the consensus of all the sections of our people. This we have managed partly because of our foreign policy. If we had sided with the West or the East, India itself would have been divided internally. Far from getting consensus for our economic and political development we would have had the country polarized between right and left from the very beginning of our independence. It would have disturbed very profoundly the stability, the unity and the peace of our country, and made it impossible for us to achieve the peaceful, planned economic development which has produced some very concrete results for our people today. So our foreign policy gave us the opportunity of keeping away from the international schism or the cold war of our time and prevented our domestic politics from becoming a reflection of the conflict of the great powers. That gave us a period of peace and equally importantly a fundamental minimum consensus in our own country on major issues. That is how our foreign policy has played an important part in our internal development and helped in the success of our democratic system.

What is it that we have achieved internally in India apart from keeping the democratic system going on? At the end of 1954 Jawaharlal Nehru visited China after the first visit of Premier Zhou en-Lai to Delhi in June 1954. Nehru had a long discussion with Chairman Mao who recieved him cordially. Mao believed that socialism was the best method for developing countries. The Chinese had earlier characterized Indian democracy as a kind of camouflaged capitalism and had doubted if democratic socialism espoused by Nehru would lead us anywhere. Mao told Nehru that they could wait and see which method, the Indian or the Chinese, would finally produce results for the people, and if the Indian mehtod succeeded, well then he would agree with Nehru.

In the realm of foreign policy it has been interesting for me to read the description of Chinese foreign policy in recent years as an "independent foreign policy" taking positions on international issues "on merits." These were phrases that Nehru also used to describe Indian foreign policy from the end of 1940s onwards. You will recall that

Chairman Mao used to say that one must lean to one side or the other and a third road did not exist. Nehru's position was that a third road did exist and we need not have to take our stand on what Moscow or Washington or Europe thought, but according to our own understanding and interests judging each issue on merits and from the point of view of what was good for world peace. Certainly one of the most refreshing developments in the world is the evolution of the foreign policy of China in recent years. I am not saying that Chinese foreign policy today is the same as ours; it is different and distinctively Chinese; but there are now more common points than before.

As you know, both China and India have done well in the economic field. In certain fields China's achievements may be greater—in heavy industries like steel, in the exploration and production of oil, in the application of nuclear energy for defence purposes, and also in the achievement of greater equality in the distribution of a minimum of essential goods to the people. India can also be proud of its achievements, even though much has yet to be achieved. What is really remarkable is that whatever progress we have made has been within the framework of a parliamentary democracy and without imposing colossal sacrifices on the people. Let us take agriculture. India today is basically self-sufficient in foodgrains, it is for the first time that this has happened in modern history. This was brought about through democratic means, gradually but systematically, by educating the farmer in modern methods of cultivation. I should like to acknowledge here the contribution made by the United States of America in this field of agricultural revolution in India—I would rate it as the one single most important and far-reaching contribution made by the U.S.A. to Indian development. Of course a great deal was done in this field by the Indian government and the people of India.

The other great internal development in India has been the transformation which has come over the industrial face of the country. It may not be very dramatic when you look at this from here from the peaks of your technological progress, but it is remarkable when you compare it with what we were like at the time of Independence, when hardly anything was manufactured in India. Today over ninety five percent of the goods used by the Indian people are produced in India and much of it is exported to other countries also. We have also built up a very variegated technological and industrial infrastructure. The World Bank has rated India as the tenth industrialized nation in the world. Of course within this larger picture we have developing areas, backward areas. I do not want to minimise the shortcomings, the lack of achievement in many fields, but the fact is that through our agricultural success and industrial and technological success we have provided a base for our development and a mechanism and a method which is democratic for further progress, for uplifting the seven hundred million people who inhabit this vast land. This peaceful democratic transformation, this on-going modernization of a vast country is really the story of modern India, a story that also enfolds the fundamental affinities in values as well as interests that exist between American democracy and the democracy of India.

XI

Youth: A World to Inherit

I am always a little perturbed when I speak to young audiences, be it in the United States or in my own country, India. There is a gap between the grown-up and the youth of today, not merely in terms of chronology and age, but psychologically, culturally and even interest-wise. Since we adults believe that the responsibility for running the world lies on our shoulders, it is logical to argue that the responsibility for overcoming this generation gap also devolves primarily upon us and our fore-fathers. It has often been said that while science and technology have advanced with bewildering speed, transcending its terrestrial bounds and reaching out to "the unreachable stars" and plumbing "the vasty deeps" of the ocean, the mind and the vision of mankind has remained earthy, narrow and pathetically self-centered and bedevilled with a thousand prejudices and misconceptions about the world and peoples

Ambassador K. R. Narayanan was the chief guest at the opening convocation of Wesley College in Dover, Delaware, on September 8, 1983. This convocation in the 111th year of the college was attended by about 500 students, faculty and members of the public. The Convocation Ceremonies were presided over by Dr. Reed Stewart, President of the College.

inhabiting other parts of this globe. What is called the generation gap is only a part of this general, gaping gap in human understanding.

I am not here to dole out advice to the eager young boys and girls who have entered the portals of this college in search of knowledge and careers. It was Oscar Wilde who quipped that: "it is always a silly thing to give advice, but to give good advice is fatal." In this tortuous, harsh, but exhilarating adventure that is life, each one of us has in the final analysis, to fall back upon one's own inclinations, intuitions, capabilities and resources and steer one's own path to progress and happiness. Therefore, one must have the freedom to explore one's own way, make one's own experiments with life, make one's own mistakes and discover one's own mission in life.

But the thrill and the joy of life is that we do this not as isolated, self-contained, individuals but as members of a family, a class, a college, a university, a society, a nation and a world. It is not reckless, self-regarding adventure, but one that takes into account and derives inspiration and strength from the aspirations, endeavours, and interests of other people. A German philosopher once said, in his pungent German way, "Yes, you have freedom to move your hand, but it is limited by the position of your neighbor's nose." Today the whole world is a vast neighborhood and the position of almost everyone's nose is our intimate concern. Therefore, freedom , the pursuit of one's self-interest and enjoyment of the good things of life, have got to be balanced by concern and feeling for others if they are to be meaningful, creative and really delightful.

We go to schools, colleges and universities for learning and for preparing ourselves for the struggles of a highly competitive society. At the same time, we do so, for developing a balanced personality and evolving a healthy outlook on life and the world. The Indian view of education was put forward by our first Prime Minister Jawaharlal Nehru, who said: " A university stands for humanism, for tolerance, for reason, for progress, for the adventure of ideas, and for the search of truth. It stands for the onward march of the human race towards ever higher objectives. If the universities discharge their duties adequately, then it is well with the nation and the people. But if the temple of learning itself becomes a home of narrow bigotry and petty objectives, how then will the nation prosper or a person grow in stature?"

In this larger context of the role of an educational institution, it is satisfying to learn that the Wesley College is now embarking upon a plan to have larger numbers of foreign students on its campus. International inter-course and understanding of other nations and peoples is necessary for colleges and universities everywhere, but it is particularly so in the United States of America. This is a nation that occupies a central position in the world in terms of wealth, knowledge, power and influence. The responsibilities attached to this world-position are enormous and awesome. It is important that the bright and intelligent youth of this great country, which would take over tomorrow or the day after tomorrow, these enormous and awesome responsibilities, should have a heightened awareness, a clearer understanding, of the complex confused but inter-dependent world in which we live, and also to have broad sympathies for the vast majority of mankind who live and struggle in conditions less easy and less fortunate than in this land of opportunity.

According to the latest statistics available, the world population today is about 4.7 billion, out of which about

234 million live in the United States. I have referred to this statistics not to conjure up before you the nightmare of a world weighed down with people, but to drive home the point that the great majority of humanity live outside the United States, and indeed outside the United States and the Soviet Union put together. The world is not exhausted by the Americans, the Russians and the Europeans, and there are other peoples with histories, interests and aspirations of their own and looking at the world with different eyes. For them bread and butter are more important than guns and missiles, and living together in peace a greater priority than the struggle for the balance of power or the balance of terror.

Another major factor of our time is world inter-dependence. The powerful and the weak, the rich and the poor, the developed and the devloping nations are all caught in this net of inter-dependence. Someone has said facetiously that communications have brought mankind so close together that it is possible today for a traveller to have "breakfast in Cairo and diarrhoea in Karachi!" More seriously, a tragedy in some remote corner of the globe can shake and shock the whole world within a matter of hours, and an error of judgement by a military commander can ignite a world war, and the mere pressing of a button by someone in a lonely room can burst the world into a terminal conflagration. It does not matter who is right and who is wrong, who is good and who is wicked; everyone can end up in nuclear annihilation and agonising radioactive destruction.

In the middle fifties, President Eisenhower saw clearly the implications of the new weapons-systems. Pointing out that "we are rapidly getting to the point that no war can be won," Eisenhower wrote: "War implies contest; when you get to the point that contest is no longer involved, and the outlook comes close to destruction of the enemy and suicide for ourselves—an outlook neither side can ignore—then arguments as to the exact amount of available strength, as compared to somebody else's are no longer the vital issues. When we get to the point, as one day we will, that both sides know that in any outbreak of general hostilities, regardless of the element of surprise, destruction will be both reciprocal and complete, possibly we will have sense enough to meet at the conference table, with the understanding that the era of armaments has ended, and the human race must conform its action to this truth, or die." The day Eisenhower envisaged has arrived when the super powers have amassed in their armouries instruments of mass destruciton that can destroy the world several times over.

It is in this context that the world heard once again through the medium of the cinema the message of Mahatma Gandhi. As you know, Gandhi preached and practised nonviolence as a philosophy and a method for dealing with the problems and conflicts that bedevil mankind. Military power today, by virtue of its sheer over-development and self-destructiveness, has become irrelevant to the solution of the basic issues of our time. The dilemma for us is that while violence has become suicidal and irrelevant, the minds and hearts of people are inflamed by passions and hatred, or as Gandhi himself put it "the eyes of the world are blood-shot with violence and hatred." I believe that at this fateful moment in history, we have to turn our minds to peace and peaceful co-existence and find ways of relieving tensions among nations so that we have a world to live in and the youth of tomorrow a world to inherit with all the brilliant prospects of prosperity and plenty opened up by the advance of science and technology.

I used the word peaceful co-existence more than once in this address. We in India have had some experience of this in our philosophy and historical practice. Though our history has had its periods of violence and conflicts as that of any other nation, we have had also a strong tradition of tolerance and co-existence which is today manifested in our democratic system of government. With its population of over 700 million, India is the largest democracy sharing a natural affinity with the United States, the most powerful and affluent democracy in the world. We have represented in India every religion of the world—while the majority are Hindus, we have over 80 million Muslims, the third largest in the world, and 14 million Christians—Christianity came to India in the first century A.D. long before the Roman Empire was converted to it. We have besides, Sikhs, Buddhists, Jains, Zoroastrians. And we have a small community of Jews who first arrived in India before the advent of the Christian era and who have known neither persecution nor discrimination in India as it has been their lot in Europe—indeed even the word anti-Semitism was unknown to us until we heard it from some of the advanced countries of Europe. You might ask me what about the religious violence some of you must have seen in the film "Gandhi." That was a tragic deviation into madness on the part of people uprooted by the partition of the country, a madness that was controlled and brought to an end by the nonviolent method of Mahatma Gandhi.

I want to say that in our long history in which we lived together with immense diversities, religious, regional, cultural, racial and linguistic, we have had nothing like the Crusades or the Thirty Years War which had ravaged Europe. This is the historical background against which our present-day policy of nonalignment must be seen *viz.* not participating in the ideological crusade of our time while believing in and maintaining our democracy, and keeping away from the political-cum-military alliances that divide the Great Powers today. We are convinced that today even more than in the past, co-existence of different religions, ideologies and political and social systems are necessary, inevitable and possible.

I have digressed into international politics. Perhaps it is not a digression but the main theme for modern history. This theme, to my mind, is at the heart of education. Plato once chided one of his interlocutors who believed politics to be dirty and beneath one's dignity to be indulged in and said: "The heaviest penalty for declining to engage in politics is to be ruled by someone inferior to yourself."

Of course, the duty of the student is to study and equip oneself for the responsibilities of life; at the same time he or she has to develop awareness and understanding of the issues that agitate mankind today.

They say this is literally a world of the young. Young people seem to predominate the composition of the population in almost every country. We have in India about 120 million boys and girls going to schools and 3.5 million going to colleges and universities. Though they study in a different part of the world, in a different cultural context, they are moved by the same urges and aspirations as you are in this advanced country. This is what constitutes the essential unity of mankind.

I have said a little while ago that the principal duty of a student is to study; study means imbibing values and standards that make knowledge meaningful and worthwhile. It also involves discipline, I should add voluntary and imaginative discipline, discipline combined with a maximum of freedom. Justice Holmes once said: "The irresistible always comes to pass through effort." I believe that those who have entered this campus are destined to play their respective important roles in the future life of this nation. But that irresistible destiny will come to pass through your efforts. May I wish your efforts every success, and wish that your life on the campus be as joyous as it is useful, to you, to your families, to your country, and to the larger world that is knocking at the doors of your consciousness for admittance and understanding.

XII
Human Capital and Education

To set myself at ease, I should like to start by quoting a rather self-deprecating statement by a British vice chancellor, the counterpart of an American president, Sir Allen Bullock, when he took over as the vice chancellor of the University of Oxford. He said, "the best academics just think; the ones who can't think, write; the ones who can't write, teach; and the ones who can't teach, become vice chancellors." I'm sure it is not enough these days just to think and meditate. We are living in a changing, dynamic world and the builders of the future, particularly of American youth gathered here, will have to ponder not only the future of the student but almost the future of the world. You have given me a very complicated and baffling subject. I shall, therefore, merely simplify it within the limited time available to me.

"Human capital" is, to my mind, a rather limited expression. The human being can be looked upon as a resource, a capital, a unit of production, but the human

International address to the 22nd Annual Meeting of the American Association of State Colleges and Universities on 31 October 1982 in Nashville, Tennessee.

being has many other dimensions. I'm sure you will be the first to agree with me that the human being has a social, cultural, and, if I may, a spiritual dimension beyond the economic dimensions in which we are all involved. In our own Indian thought, we have always considered the self-development of the individual—self-improvement, self-fulfillment—as one of the great objectives of education.

In our own time, of course, we have to link this to scientific and technological advance. But if you do not link this together and keep pace with one another, then we would face a very jarring and dangerous dichotomy. Our Prime Minister, Jawaharlal Nehru, who was also somewhat of a thinker, talked about science and technology and said that "science which has destroyed many gods has itself assumed the posture of a god." It is trying to create almost a new superstition and subjugate man to its own logic. And he asked "are there not other dimensions to human life?" He said science has not dealt with the ultimate purposes of life, which he characterized as the desire "to gain knowledge, to realize truth, and to appreciate goodness and beauty."

I think this is a goal which education has to propagate. It is really nothing new because some of the great scientists have also adhered to the same view of science and of man. Einstein once said "concern for man himself and his fate must always form the chief interest of all technical endeavour, concern for the great unsolved problems of the organization of labor and the distribution of goods in order that the creations of our minds shall be a blessing and not a curse to mankind." We are today in an age when the creations of the minds of man have opened up almost a cornucopia for human beings. But, at the same time, it can be a curse to mankind unless through education, through training, we are able to control the forces released by technology and use them for really human and humane purposes.

Now, there are, I think, two or three aspects of education. One would be the scientific technological process—that is, to achieve the mastery of nature and the objective world. The second one is, to my mind, social constructiveness, and the third is cultural, psychological self-development. It is quite easy for mankind to separate these three aspects and pursue one alone.

Yesterday, I was listening, with immense interest, to the lecture by the chairman of the Control Data Corporation. He talked about the great invention of PLATO—the computer. It is absolutely essential to utilize this for human purposes, social purposes, and for further educational and scientific expansion. At the same time, it is necessary to go back to the old Plato—if I may say so—who thought about wisdom, the need for wisdom, the need for patience, the need for understanding human nature.

Human nature, strangely, has not changed very much over thousands and thousands of years. It requires great trials, joys, sorrows, failures, and tragedies for human nature to mature and to become a refined civilized thing. And even when we have achieved this civilized state, only a little partition stands between it and the unleashing of what I call barbarism. The old days were, I think very barbarous days. Wars were fought, but there were duels by the leaders and that settled the business. Now I'm not sure if we are really more civilized today when the leaders sit in very comfortable places and send to the battlefield thousands and thousands of young people who fight for them and the causes they espouse. But the nature of the whole conflict has changed in this world. And, hence, I think we have to understand this nature of the human being, the fashioning of it and the direction of it towards constructive purposes while not shunning the great blessings, the great opportunities, given to us by science and technology, because science and technology are really the most magnificent products of the human mind. We cannot run away from them; we should not run away from them. We should utilize them and direct them to our human and social and global purposes.

Years ago, I came across a quotation about war by one of the great leaders of a major war, World War I. The author is none other than Winston Churchill. It is really amazing to read it now. He said this in 1929 and I should like to read it because if I produce any other quotation of a similar kind it may be suspect. Churchill said, "The disproportion between the quarrels of nations and the suffering which fighting out those quarrels involves; the poor and the barren prizes which reward sublime endeavour on the battlefield; the fleeting triumph of war; the long slow rebuilding; the awful risk so hardily run, the doom missed by a hair's breadth, by the spin of a coin, by the accident of an accident—all this should make the prevention of another war the main preoccupation of mankind." He said it in 1929 and he fought a major war—World War II—which he called the "unnecessary war." Now I think this great quotation from Churchill is applicable with even greater force to our own times. And, indeed this has been one of the strongly held beliefs of India as a nation—that the major task before us is to prevent another world conflict. And education, the training of young people and their minds, has to be in this direction. One has to think not of war, as Nehru put it, but think of peace; not prepare for war, but prepare for peace. If you think of war and prepare for it, there is a likelihood of its happening.

Now, it is alright for me to preach in this way, but I should like to say one thing—the experiences and study of history as well as the compulsions of technology have shown the need for coexistence. In my own country, we have a very complex, diverse history where almost all the great religions of the world are represented. Innumerable languages are spoken; there are different cultural patterns, different types of food and dress; and somehow, though not easily, we have managed to coexist together and to work together for a larger purpose.

If you look also at the world as a whole, you will find that great revolutions have taken place, great religious and ideological movements have taken place, but the world remains today multireligious, multiideological. When Christianity developed in the world, some great powers were behind this Christian religion. It spread but then it settled down; other religions coexisted. Islam had a very spectacular spread in the world but then the momentum stopped at a certain time and people settled down. The same thing has happened to ideologies, and the world is, in fact, a multireligious, multiideological place. It has been so for centuries and we have to understand this so that we do not try to change it in the hope that the world can be made some kind of a monolithic place where one religion or one ideology or one system only will prevail.

I think that the major task of education is to convey this predicament of mankind, that we have to accept differences and live with them and learn to cooperate at the same time. I don't know what diplomacy has to do with it. I think that because I am an Ambassador you expect me to say something about it in my speech. I think that academics probably have more to do with the fashioning of the world than diplomats. A diplomat, as someone put it, is one who practices the law of specific levitation—that is, tries to keep his head above water and pretend that he is directing the course of events. But diplomacy has also developed new dimensions. Today it is not only bilateral relations in which nations indulge. Every bilateral relation has an international and even a global dimension.

You have heard about the North-South dialogue, the great question of the relationship between developing and developed nations. When I think of my country's relationship with this great country of the United States, I feel that in that is focused the entire issue of the relations between the developing nations and the developed nations. The United States has reached the greatest peak of development. India is the paragon of a developing nation. Our relationship is a fairly good example of the interdependence of nations in the world. As everybody knows technology has made the world one, and in fact it was in this country that the ideal of one world was projected in a modern political form for the first time, when Presidnet Wilson said that we are no longer provincials.

Wendell Wilkie talked about a one world, and this one world, as a result of the development of technology is much more realistic today than ever before. Consider the great economic sickness of our time—every country is going through some sort of a recession, some sort of unemployment, and all manner of problems. One may ask—are all these just accidental or are there more profound reasons for them? Many people have analyzed this situation. We in the developing world are dependent to a great extent on the advanced, developed world. At the same time, the developed world is also really dependent on us.

I can make a very audacious statement: that the

economies of the advanced countries, which are stagnating today, where the rate of growth is slow, where unemployment is increasing, will not, or are not likely, to get opportunities for fuller employment and more rapid growth unless there is much more intercourse, interchange, transfer of wealth, and transfer of technology to the vast majority of people in the world who live in the so-called Third World. The markets of the future are there. Without these markets, I think the economic growth of the advanced countries might come to a dead end unless these resources and opportunities available in the Third World are harnessed and developed, and unless there is more equitable sharing of resources and transfer of science and technology from the developed to the developing countries.

We depend on each other not only for constructive purposes, but are involved in a destructive process as well; there can be no isolated destruction in a future world war. As Jawaharlal Nehru once put it, "the world faces either coexistence or codestruction." I do not have to dwell upon this, because I am sure as those who think about these problems and think about the future of the younger generation, it is already in all your minds. But one has to analyze why there is this distemper among people today— why even in a very affluent, advanced, highly educated society like that of the United States there is such distemper and increase of crime and of other social ills. It is not just an aberration. I have a feeling that when you have before you the threat of a nuclear disaster, at least as a possibility, with nothing very much being done about it by the great nations of the world—because at the moment we are hurtling to disaster—accumulating more and more weapons of destruction, using science and technology for militarizing space, militarizing the oceans of the world, and are not really engaged in a resolution of the armament race, I think it is quite natural for people to feel in their subconscious that their future is limited, risky, and uncertain. And this uncertainty, probably, in a psychological sense, has released a certain sense of irresponsibility among people, and hence the great need not only to avert a cataclysm, but also in order to stabilize our own societies, to think and talk about problems of war and peace and to give some direction and some hope to young people, so that all these magnificent achievements of science and technology are directed for solving the problems on earth, the common problems of mankind and not for a competition under the sea or in space. We are thus involved in an adventure in interdependence to which, I think, educators have much to contribute in the sense of arousing world consciousness and creating understanding between peoples. Intellectual cooperation is one of the major forces behind such world consciousness and understanding.

If I may for a moment talk about my country and your country—I think the degree of intellectual cooperation between India and the United States is something which neither Indians nor the people in the United States fully realize. There are thousands and thousands of students here—not only today but for the last 30 or 40 or 50 years and there are many scientists, doctors, professors here who absorb values and who have transmitted them to India and vice-versa. And this cooperation in the intellectual field is an area that had been expanding.

As regards human capital, to the best of our ability we have tried to direct our attention to the building of this human capital for our future. What I am trying to emphasize is that it is this intellectual link that has enabled our two countries to remain friendly with one another and cooperate with one another in a very significant way even when we had many periods of misunderstandings and zigs and zags in our relationship. This academic, intellectual cooperation has sustained us, and I think it is the most enduring basis of not only Indo-American relations but of relations of countries of all the world. And this gathering here is a splendid example of this cooperation. I want to thank you and pay tribute to the Association for bringing all of us together in this room, which is a miniature kind of international academia. Thank you very much.

XIII

India in the Global Society

I am grateful to you for giving me this opportunity to exchange views with the members of this very prestigious and influential institution. I am aware of the importance of this think tank on the West Coast—power has been shifting to this part of the United States!

I am very attracted by the use of the word 'global society', because I think the phrase itself is a compassionate phrase in the world of today. As far as India is concerned, it had always a world outlook and was involved in world developments. India has received much from the rest of the world and absorbed, digested and transformed these world influences trying to integrate them into our society and into our philosophy. In turn India has also contributed quite a bit to the world. In fact, when I was in China, I was surprised to see for myself the influence Buddhism had on China. When I went around, I could see the imprint of India in the temples and rock carvings and in some of the institutions which survived even the cultural revolution. I found Sanskrit written in all manner of unexpected places

A discussion at the Robert Maynard Hutchins Centre for the Study of Democratic Institutions, Santa Barbara, on April 13, 1981.

in China, in Beijing, Chungtu, Chunking, Sian, Loyang etc.
India too had received a lot from China in terms of ideas, art
forms and articles of daily use.

Right from the beginning, India had developed a world
outlook, almost a universal view. Indians, even two thousand
years ago, thought in universal terms as if there was
something like a global society even in those ancient times.
That, of course, is an old story but part of the old story
continues in our present day thinking, in our present day
attitude to problems of the world. The central tradition in
India has been one of toleration. You cannot have a global
view unless you have the spirit of tolerance, the willingness
to look at other peoples, other civilizations, other societies
with a tolerant and understanding eye rather than with an
attitude of strangeness or conflict.

We have not only diversity in our society but we believe
that diversity is an essential part of life. I recall that Pandit
Nehru once said that many conquerors had tried to conquer
the world and to produce some monolithic system out of it.
They failed, whether they were military conquerors or
religious conquerors. Great religions have arisen and spread
in the world like wild fire but we still have a multi-religious
world. No religion has succeeded in wiping out another.

In the same way in our modern times new ideologies
have emerged, aggressive ideologies, and tried to overwhelm other ideologies through political and even military
methods; but we still have a multi-ideological world.

It was out of this world view that we fashioned, soon
after our independence, what we call the policy of nonalignment and peaceful co-existence. It is not a policy of
standing aloof from others on the ground that a certain
system is evil, and therefore, we should not associate
ourselves with it. We may be nonaligned with one or the

other bloc, but we believe in co-existence with both. As a matter of fact, we cannot survive as a nation if there is no co-existence among different religions and groups that constitute India. It is this very approach that we have adopted to the rest of the world; in a sense India is actually a microcosm of the world. That is how we came to the conclusion at the very inception of the cold war that our role in the world was to contribute, as much as we can, to understanding between conflicting blocs and to play a reconciliatory role between them. Of course, we are not a big power, we do not have any great economic strength or any great military strength. But to the extent we can pull any weight in the world, we wanted to put it on the scale of peace and understanding. We thought that it was particularly important to do so after the appearance of deadly nuclear weapons backing the ideological confrontation in the world.

We believed that people were not as evil or as irreconcilably antagonistic as it was made out to be, whether they are Russians or Chinese or Americans. They are all caught in the same planet and have to live together whether they like it or not. Jawaharlal Nehru in one of his statements in the middle fifties after his visit to the Soviet Union, said that he was struck by the similarity between the Americans and Russians. He said that both had tremendous vitality, and both wanted to express themselves somehow in a grand way; both believed in science and technology more than any other people in the world, and both wanted to develop it in a very grandiose manner. At the same time both were plagued by a sense of insecurity in spite of all their power and were constantly trying to upstage or overwhelm each other. Out of this fear all manner of repercussions followed not only for themselves but for the rest of the world.

Franklin Roosevelt once said that fear was the only thing to be feared. I think we are now in such a situation. Today this great country, which has no economic peer, and which, in spite of all that is being talked about the military balance, enjoys military, scientific and technological superiority in the world, receives shockwaves of nervousness running from Administration to media, from media to people when governmental changes not to its liking take place somewhere even in a small country. This kind of exaggerated fear strikes the Soviet Union also.

We in India opted for the policy of nonalignment and peaceful co-existence in order to help create a slightly more peaceful world—let us not talk about an ideal world—in which people can live with greater ease of mind and without the fear of being annihilated by falling nuclear bombs. India happens to be a very important strategic mass in Asia. By taking this geographical mass out of the vortex of great power conflict, we were helping in the lessening of tensions, preventing the accentuation of tensions and adding at the same time to what might have appeared a negative policy of nonalignment, positive policies of co-existence and co-operation. The strategic importance of this role of India is rarely understood. When people describe India's nonalignment as a pro-Soviet policy, I sometimes ask: "Suppose the seven hundred million people of India were really pro-Soviet, suppose India were really pursuing internal and external policies which were pro-Soviet, what would have been the strategic situation in Asia today?"

What we have done is not to have joined up with the Soviet Union or with the United States in the military-strategic confrontation. We have not sided in this way with the USA in spite of many moral, cultural and political affinities we have with it. That is because of our belief that nonalignment was the best policy with which we could help peace in our region and in the world by creating an area of relative tranquility, an area of stability, in which Americans and the Soviets are not engaged actively and directly in a struggle against each other. As a result, we have gained some sense of security which is, to my mind, valuable to the Soviet Union and perhaps even more to the United States. One can understand this if one takes note of the fact how a toppling of a regime or a sudden internal change even in a small country stirs up a lot of talk here of sending arms, military advisers, economic aid etc. to salvage U.S. interests there. The democratic system and the political stability we have managed to establish in India, and the foreign policy we have followed, are such that India does not create any strategic headaches either to the United States or to the Soviet Union. So we are by and large left alone, though each super power may believe that it would be better to have India on its side. However, our own analysis is that if India were on one side or the other, that would lead to greater tension and conflict in the world, and what is more it might well result in internal struggles and conflicts within India itself.

India is a huge country with a large population, with colossal problems, problems of poverty and social inequality. In such a situation if there arose polarization within the country, which could be the case if we joined one bloc or the other, we would have faced major domestic dissensions and differences. We feared that once that happened in a huge society, then things would go out of control. We know that when the Chinese liberation war was going on the United States sank enormous amounts of money and armaments to help Chiang kai-Shek. But that could not save Chiang and his regime. Not because of the aid given by Stalin—he gave precious little to the Chinese communists as we know now—but because of the efforts of the Chinese themselves who felt they were fighting for something, fighting for their liberation and for changing their social order. So the assistance to Chiang kai-Shek was of no avail. Thus in a poor and populous country any polarization, in my opinion, would help only leftist forces and not western democracy. No intervention and help from outside could then save the situation. That is why the main emphasis in India has been on economic and social development and on creating some sort of a consensus in our society on major internal and external issues. It is through foreign policy, through economic planning, and democracy that we managed to produce a working consensus in our society.

One may ask how India managed to maintain the democratic system, while other countries next to us like Pakistan which had the same historical experience and the same British tutelage, could not maintain it. There are several countries which were ruled by the British and where the British had built up at least some semi-parliamentary institutions during the colonial period but which were discarded with great ease within five or ten years of getting their independence. Was it by mere accident that India managed to maintain and develop its democracy in difficult circumstances involving the passing away of the first generation of leaders, then the death of our second Prime Minister in office, and later a change in power from the historic Congress Party to a new party and recently the return of the Congress to power again under Mrs. Gandhi— all these through the democratic process of elections? Therefore, democracy in India is not just a fragile experiment. It is a settled political pattern.

It has been possible for us to achieve this for four reasons. Mahatma Gandhi once said, after wholeheartedly acknowledging the contribution made by the British, that it was possible for democracy to grow in India because its roots were present in Indian social institutions like the panchayats; the panchayats were self-governing village institutions which practised from ancient days some democratic forms for managing their affairs. It was these old traditions that helped in sustaining modern democracy—there was some sort of remembered basis for it in the grass roots. Another reason was, as I mentioned earlier, the central tradition of toleration.

A third reason was that the leaders of the Indian nationalist movement, Mahatma Gandhi, Jawaharlal Nehru and others believed in democracy very passionately. For them it was not just a British imposition. In fact, if you study the history of the Indian nationalistic movement, you will find it was the Indians who were asking for democratic rights. The struggle for independence was also a demand for democratic freedoms from Britain almost in the same way as the American demand for independence began with the cry of "no taxation without representation." The early Indian nationalist leaders said that as Indians were British subjects, citizens of the Empire, they should have the same freedoms as the British. Thus the liberal concept of democracy developed in India even before Gandhiji gave it a revolutionary mass basis. The Indian nationalist leadership was committed to democracy over a long period. On the other hand, Mohammed Ali Jinnah, the founder of Pakistan, had argued that parliamentary democracy was a foreign institution which could never be applied to conditions in Asia, especially in India. The result was that while Pakistani leaders did not or could not try very much to develop these institutions after independence, the Indian leadership deliberately tried to develop them.

There was a fourth reason which made democracy sustain itself in India. We tried to apply the democratic system, the democratic method for economic and social development. Democracy would not have been accepted by the people merely because they thought it was good in theory. It would be accepted by a people only if they believed that it could provide answers to their crying needs.

It was for the first time in history that what is called a legislative state emerged in India, a state which legislated reform for changing society and for removing inequalities and social injustices. In other words, we used the democratic system, the Parliament, and the methods of discussion and debate for bringing about an economic and social transformation. This introduced into democracy a new meaning for the common people.

In my view these are some of the main reasons why we managed to provide for ourselves a democratic framework. It is not a slender coating applied from outside.

It is, I think, difficult to understand Indian foreign policy without understanding Indian democracy. Our outlook on the world and our involvement in the global society are conditioned by it. Notwithstanding many shortcomings and mistakes, what we have tried to follow is the vision of India as part of a world community.

(The above opening remarks were followed by a session of questions and answers.)

Q: What role do you think India could play in working towards a political expression in the form of world law for this global society?

A: I am not very knowledgeable about international legal issues, but I know that we have been working in various fora, particularly in the United Nations, to help the evolution of a system of laws for the world as a whole. In the field of international law and diplomacy we played a part in the conclusion of the Vienna Agreements. We are very deeply involved in the Law of the Sea Conference. The sea will be a very important source of wealth in the future. Even now there is almost a scramble under the sea for these resources. We believe that it is important to preserve the freedom of the seas and also to have laws for the exploitation of the wealth of the seas. We have an important oceanographic programme. Only a few weeks ago I read that one of our ships has scooped up multi-metallic modules from the seabed, rich in several types of minerals including traces of gold. So, you can see what is involved in all this. In fact, our legal experts have contributed to the negotiations at the Law of the Sea Conference. Outer space is another area where we have been working for an international agreement.

Q: The present U.S. Administration has decided to suspend all approaches towards a Law of the Sea which had been converging towards some possible, decent overall decision. Would it be part of Indian foreign policy to feel strongly enough to rebuke the present Administration for doing that?

A: Well, we feel that by rebuking we reach nowhere! The great powers particularly do not like to be rebuked, by each other or by smaller countries. So, we have to adopt methods which are more constructive and can produce results. We hope that all that the Administration has said is that they would like to look at the Law of the Sea afresh. It is our hope that after they have examined it afresh they would come to more or less the same conclusions which have been reached by the consensus of nations.*

Q: You have spent some years in China. India and China have always struck me as being in many ways at opposite ends of a spectrum of different paths of development. How do you, and Indians in general, view the Chinese path to development? Do you believe that this is something that is somehow perhaps culturally determined or do developing countries really have much of a choice to decide whether they want to go a pluralistic route or whether they want to do it with the kind of regimentation that China has gone through?

A: In India we adopted a different method of development. I recall that when Jawaharlal Nehru visited China in 1954, he had a discussion with Chairman Mao tse-Tung at the end of which Mao said that the two countries could go their separate ways in development and we would finally see who did better. We adopted the democratic method because we believed in it. Nehru made a very important speech in the middle fifties under the title: "The Basic Approach." It put across his philosophy of development. He held the view that the human being was at the centre of things and that the democratic method of development, in the long run, would bring more enduring results than development imposed from the top through totalitarian methods.

China has made great progress. In certain fields they have made greater progress than we have—they have achieved a great deal for their people. As you know they have nuclear bombs, they have missiles. However, in the

Finally the U.S. Administration did not sign the Treaty.

development of nuclear energy for civilian, non-military purposes we are much more advanced than China. We have also developed a space programme for peaceful purposes in a slow but steady way. We are today not far behind China in certain respects and are ahead of China in certain other respects. One field in which we are strong is the number of scientists and technologists we have today. This pool was built up not as a crash programme but over a long period of education, giving people freedom to choose their disciplines and vocations. China today has an ambitious programme for science education and technological development. They have some excellent scientists of top quality, but I think there might be a shortage at intermediate levels in regard to scientists, technicians and managers.

Q: Are you prepared for all the social and other effects of science and technology after your development?

A: We believe very intensely in science and technology. Just because it has been used for evil or warlike purposes does not mean that we should turn our backs on science and technology. We have reached a stage where some of our problems, the world's problems, cannot be solved without the application of science and technology. Whether one uses or misuses them is a matter of choice, a matter of policy. There is no inevitability about the development of nuclear energy leading to the manufacture of nuclear weapons. There is a strong case for using it for peaceful constructive purposes. It all depends on your policies, on what you want to do. But I should like to say that we have no blind faith in science and technology, nor do we give any unbalanced importance for its development. As a proportion of our national budget we spend very little on it. We believe in a balance between technology and humanity, between physical sciences and social sciences. In our planning and economic development we have given great importance to agriculture, small scale industries and cottage industries. We believe that by linking modern technology with the cultural roots and refinements of an ancient society like that of India we can ultimately produce a more humane society. Modernization without abandoning our old culture is possible. But I feel that if we discard science, India might go down again as it did in the past.

Q: I have a rather philosophical question, which I would like to formulate in a very blunt way. Is it ultimately possible to have a neutral position in the world theatre? If India chooses the path of science and technology because it feels that only science and technology can solve her problems, is it not choosing something that perhaps does not do justice to the old Indian history in which, it would seem, science and technology in the modern sense of the term, are not natural to the Indian mind?

A: Your question is both philosophical and practical. As regards neutrality, I agree with you that it is not possible to be neutral on the great issues of life. Let me say that India's nonalignment is not neutrality. We are not neutral, be it in the realm of values or politics. At home we have chosen the peaceful democratic system. There is no neutrality about it. Nor are we neutral in world politics. Nonalignment involves making one's own judgements and not adopting the judgements of an ally or a bloc. If a country follows a policy simply because that is the line of its Soviet ally then that country is subordinating its own judgement to that of a great power. In the same way if a country follows the United States policy say in Africa, the Middle East, Asia or Europe simply because it is U.S.

policy, then again it is not following its own judgement in foreign policy. India is an ancient nation. We have evolved our own patterns of thinking over the ages. To think on one's own and judge issues oneself is not against scientific approach. Incidentially, India was advanced in logic, mathematics, astronomy, etc., indeed in the industry and technology of the time until she came under colonial rule.

Q: You said that one of the strengths of India's policy of nonalignment is its universality. To my mind, it seems that the two countries which are most likely to benefit from nonalignment are the United States and Russia. But would it not be a contradiction in terms to imagine that these two countries are nonaligned?

A: In an interview to the editor of an Indian weekly, Nehru once said—I think it was in the early sixties—that the nonaligned movement could never be a bloc, or represent an alignment among the nonaligned. He said that he wanted the ideas of peace and co-existence to penetrate the minds of people everywhere including the countries that are now aligned. He envisaged the final dissolution of the blocs leading to real cooperation among nations. So, even the United States and the Soviet Union are not beyond redemption as far as nonalignment is concerned! We feel that the attitude of alignment is an exclusive attitude, an attitude of conflict, because one is aligned against some other system or group. Thus if you want world cooperation, you have got to move ultimately out of the bloc system towards a global society, a global order. Jawaharlal Nehru had envisaged that nonaligned India could be an area where the United States and the Soviet Union could co-exist and compete with each other peacefully and realize finally that it is possible for them to cooperate with one another for the good of the world. I don't think that anybody can say that such a dream is unnecessary or impossible. Both the United States and the Soviet Union have reached the pinnacle of military power, neither can subjugate the other, both have to cooperate with each other.

Q: After the death of Sanjay Gandhi, the call went out from some people in the Congress Party in India for his brother Rajiv to take up his political mantle, so to speak. This has led to comments that the people of India, despite their democratic traditions, have a weakness for family or dynastic traditions. Do you agree?

A: By being democratic does not mean we are some sort of an abstract society. But India does not believe in any kind of dynastic rule. Sanjay Gandhi was a personality in himself. He organised the youth for his party, and carved out a certain position for himself in the country. Now his brother has entered politics. As far as I know, Rajiv Gandhi was quite reluctant to go into politics. He was gradually persuaded to come in. That he should help his mother is not abnormal. Had we followed the dynastic practice, Mrs. Gandhi should have taken over as Prime Minister when Nehru died. But that did not happen. It was Lal Bahadur Shastri who became the Prime Minister. He died, unfortunately, in Tashkent. After his death, the Congress leaders looked for someone around whom there could be a consensus. The party elected Mrs. Gandhi as leader and she became the Prime Minister in 1966. Don't forget that in the 1977 elections she was voted out of office and an opposition group came to power. In 1980 they went to the polls and lost and Mrs. Gandhi returned to power. These facts disprove the charge that the people of India choose their Prime Ministers on the dynastic principle. It is true that the Nehru family has an advantage as it has a record of sacrifice for the country right from the time of Motilal Nehru, the grandfather of Mrs. Gandhi, and it has established a reputation for all-India acceptability. The Nehru family has not been identified with any regional or communal group which is an advantage in a complex country like India. In the ultimate analysis, it is the people who decide. Anybody can become the Prime Minister but only through a vast process of general elections, in which people from all parts of India, Kerala, Tamilnadu, West Bengal, Punjab, Maharashtra, etc., choose the members of Parliament. The majority party in Parliament chooses its leader who becomes the Prime Minister. There is no other way a person can become the Prime Minister of India. Anybody who can pass this test can reach the top.

Q: You have described very eloquently why you feel India has been successful in maintaining its democratic posture. But as a scientist, I have to ask you an opposite question. What in your opinion are the problems that could move India to a totalitarian system?

A: I would not like to speculate on such a sordid possibility: it is most unlikely. The question of totalitarianism or any other alternative political system can arise in India only if the present system conspicuously failed, over a period of time, to meet the minimum expectations of the people. If people felt that the present system cannot deliver the goods, cannot keep law and order, cannot improve economic conditions or defend the country, then people would look for an alternative. Ultimately people do not go not so much by what might be good in theory as by what is effectively useful in fulfilling their needs. Therefore, Indian democracy will have to pass the test of efficaciousness. I think it has met the test.

Q: There have been ups and downs in India's relationship with the U.S.A. How are our relations today? I ask this question because when I visited India in 1972, I found it somewhat difficult to talk to Indian officials who seemed to be very wary of American policies and programmes.

A: The strains and tensions that you mention are luckily behind us today. I do not face any difficulty in discussing matters with U.S. officials in the State Department or the Defence Department or any other. Nor do American diplomats in India. I think the memoirs of Henry Kissinger give a clue to the reasons for the strain in Indo-U.S. relations during the period you mentioned. You are aware how the United States tilted towards Pakistan during the Bangladesh crisis and how there was an expectation in Washington that China would move in if India went into Bangladesh. You would agree that it was a grim situation for a country like India. It was a reversal of the role of the United States in regard to India. Let us also not forget that at that time the U.S. sent a Naval Task Group with a nuclear armed aircraft carrier to the Bay of Bengal. The Indian people could not understand such actions especially when India had not done anything against the interests of the United States, and when we were overwhelmed by ten million refugees coming into West Bengal. I think the diplomacy which the U.S. followed at that time was not in the stream of traditional American policy towards the region. I should like to consider it an aberration. It was during this period of great misunderstanding and resentment against U.S. policy that you went to India. Probably some of the officials you met reflected this resentment, although I must say that that was contrary to the normal Indian tradition. We have always talked to people even when they hurt us. We talked to the Chinese during and after 1962. We maintained diplomatic relations with them, and we supported their entry into the United Nations even in the year 1962. I believe your personal experience with some of our officials in 1972 was due to the then existing misunderstanding in Indo-U.S. relations. I should like to suggest to you to come to India again.

Q: What is the attitude of the Congress Party itself towards such Indian foreign policy concerns like nonalignment etc.?

A: As a party, the Congress is committed to nonalignment. You are aware that some groups have broken away from the Congress Party led by Mrs. Gandhi, but all of them accept nonalignment. It is in fact the Congress Party which adopted the idea of nonalignment through Jawaharlal Nehru. It retains its commitment to that policy. Of course, even other Indian political parties in India accept nonalignment. The Janata Party that was in power in India for two years or so also followed the policy of nonalignment although they tried to make some modifications. So, there is by and large a consensus on this policy.

Q: There is a related question. Does the Congress Party accept fully the democratic process, the democratic dogma?

A: Certainly it does, unequivocally. The Congress Party has been the ruling Party in India, except for a short period, and it has operated the democratic system in India since Independence.

XIV
Space Research and Developing Countries

It was with great pleasure as well as with a sense of awe that I accepted the invitation to inaugurate this exhibition on the Indian space programme in this historic building of the United Nations. The infinity of space still frightens us as it did early scientists like Pascal, and the attempt of man to conquer space is both awesome and exciting. Jawaharlal Nehru, the inspirer of India's scientific development, once said that science, having destroyed many a god, has itself assumed a god-like pose. It is in this context of science as a new destiny, that one looks with admiration, upon the farseeing endeavour of the United Nations to encourage and at the same time introduce law and order, in the activities of nations in the depths of the ocean and in the infinity of space and outer space.

This exhibition, as you know, has been organised as a part of a series of exhibitions in connection with the Second United Nations Conference on Outer Space. During the Conference itself, we will have in Vienna an Indian exhibition that is much more extensive.

Speech inaugurating the Exhibition on the Indian Space Programme at the United Nations Headquarters on March 3, 1982.

157

We in India eagerly look forward to this Conference, which we hope, will produce results that will ensure a fairer distribution of the benefits of the mastery of space, to all countries and to all mankind. We are happy and proud that Dr. Yashpal has been chosen as Secretary General of the Conference, which is a tribute to him as a scientist, an internationalist and a distinguished Indian.

It has sometimes been asked why a developing country like India should devote its scarce resources to such newfangled enterprises as nuclear reactors, space satellites, and Antarctic expeditions, when considerable number of our people live on the margins of existence. Dr. Vikram Sarabhai, the founder of India's space programme, answered this question when he said, "There are some who question the relevance of space activities in a developing nation. To us, there is no ambiguity of purpose. We do not have the fantasy of competing with economically advanced nations in the exploration of the moon, of the planets or manned space flights, but we are convinced that if we are to play a meaningful role nationally and in the community of nations, we must be second to none in the application of advanced technologies to the real problems of man and society, which we find in our country." That is why the thrust of our space programme is in the fields of tele-communications, mass education and instruction and meteorological research, all of which have direct relevance to the basic needs of a vast developing society.

The problems of our people are of such magnitude and complexity, and caused by arrested economic, scientific and technological development, that most of them are amenable to solutions only by a combination of social, economic and technological knowhow. Our predicament in the developing countries is such that, paradoxically, we have to reach out to the stars in order to improve our lot on this earth; it is necessary for us to climb the commanding heights of science and technology if we are to give to the millions of our people the benefits of even smaller technology. Small technology, intermediate technology and high technology are all appropriate for our development if judiciously chosen and applied. It is also important for us not to be left behind in the second and third industrial-technological revolutions as we had been in the first one. If the era of colonialism was marked by the industrial and technological superiority of the West, today at the heart of the North-South division and the struggle for a New International Economic Order is the wide disparity between developed and developing nations in the field of scientific and technological progress. This exhibition is one example of the efforts being made by the developing countries to reduce this gap and to gain a degree of self-reliance.

India's space programme is dedicated to peaceful and constructive purposes and has been undertaken in the context of international cooperation. The United Nations and its organs have played a catalytic role in this programme beginning with the sponsorship of our rocket range in Thumba back in 1966. The UN helped us in several projects including the setting up of an experimental satellite communication earth-station. Our programme has benefitted a great deal as a result of assistance from the advanced countries. The European Space Agency and the Soviet Union provided us with launchers for our satellites; the United States of America allowed us the use of its ATS-6 spacecraft for a year, and we used the Symphony Satellite of France, and the Federal Republic of Germany also for a year.

India has taken a number of parallel steps aimed at our

specific needs and general goals. We undertook major application experiments, the most well-known of which was the Satellite Instructional Television Experiment (SITE). We also carried out a number of communications experiments using the Franco-German Symphony Satellite. These efforts will culminate in the INSAT system which will provide direct television broadcast, telecommunications and meteorological services on an operational basis. The INSAT satellite is to be launched in early April by NASA in USA.

Simultaneously, we have begun the development of space hardware. Our first satellite was launched using a Soviet rocket in 1975 and since then we have launched our satellites using Soviet and European rockets. We also developed our own rockets—SLV-3 which can launch small satellites of the 80 kg. class into low earth orbits. Further, work is being done in the field of space hardware, which will lead to a semi-operational remote-sensing satellite to be launched in 1985, and more powerful rockets with a capability to launch a 600 kg. satellite. We are also envisaging the building of our own INSAT-like satellites in the future.

As I said earlier, these space efforts of ours are dedicated to peaceful purposes and to cooperation among nations. It is not a non-peaceful exploit, if I may quote Shakespeare, "of man, proud man . . . who like an angry ape . . . plays such fantastic tricks before high heaven as make the angels weep." It is, on the other hand, a part of man's efforts, to use the words of Mahatma Gandhi, "to wipe every tear from every eye" in those regions of the world where the majority of humanity lives and where again in the words of Gandhi, "life is an eternal vigil or an eternal trance." I am not trying to exaggerate the importance of our modest achievements, or to blow up the significance of this small exhibition, but if this exhibition signifies anything it is as a symbol of the aspirations and potentialities of peoples in the developing world, and also of the prospects of cooperation among nations, especially the developed and developing nations. It is, therefore, appropriate that this exhibition is held at the Headquarters of the United Nations. I have great pleasure to inaugurate it.